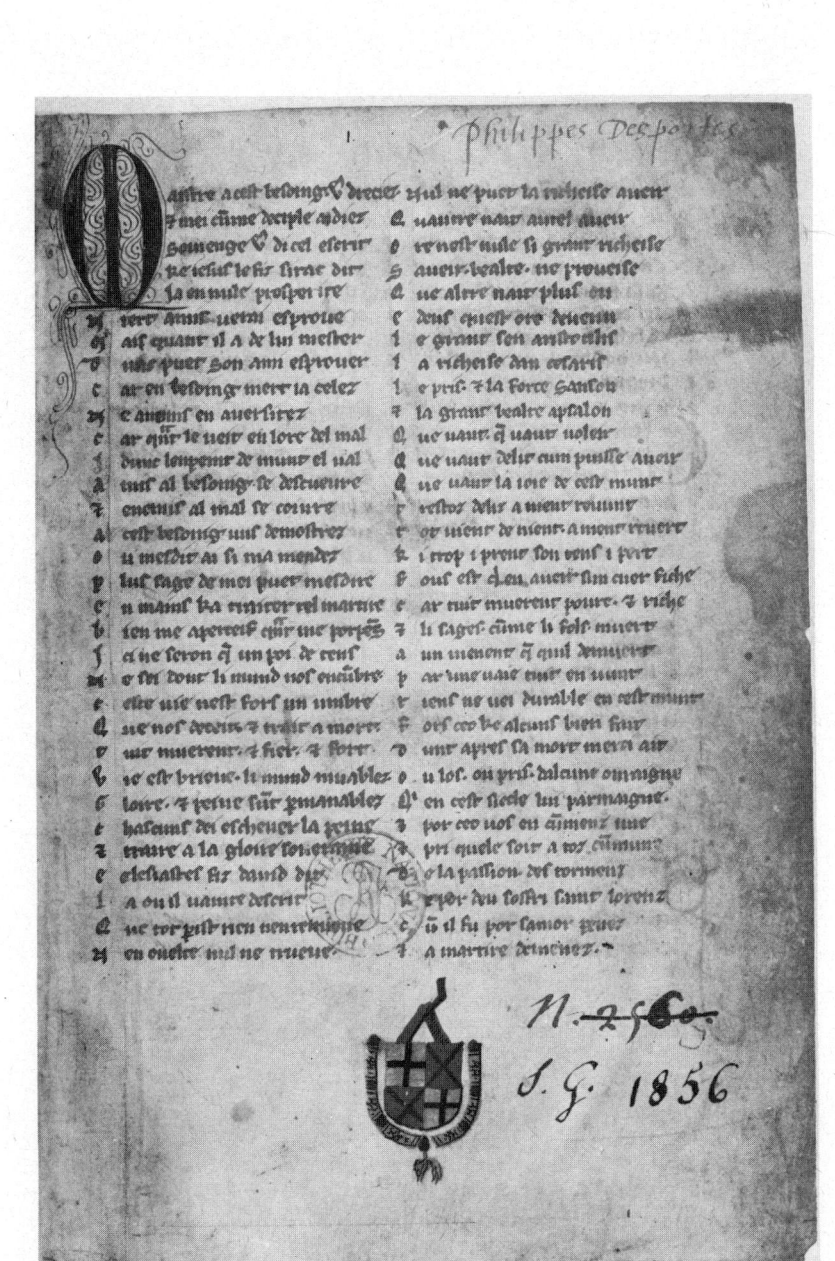

Paris, Bibliothèque Nationale, MS. fr. 19525, fol. 1ʳ, ll. 1–64.

ANGLO-NORMAN TEXTS

LA VIE DE SAINT LAURENT
AN ANGLO-NORMAN POEM
OF THE TWELFTH CENTURY

Edited by
D. W. RUSSELL

LONDON
Published and distributed by the
ANGLO-NORMAN TEXT SOCIETY
from Westfield College, London, NW3 7ST
1976

Set in IBM Baskerville
and printed in Great Britain by
Express Litho Service (Oxford)
and bound by
Kemp Hall Bindery, Oxford.

CONTENTS

ABBREVIATIONS AND SHORT TITLES

A.N.T.S.   Anglo-Norman Text Society.

Brendan   E. G. R. Waters, ed. *The Anglo-Norman Voyage of St. Brendan.* Oxford, 1928.

Gdfr.   Frédéric Godefroy. *Dictionnaire de l'ancienne langue française et de tous ses dialectes du IXe au XVe siècle.* 10 vols. Paris, 1880-1902.

Horn   Thomas. *The Romance of Horn by Thomas*, ed. M. K. Pope, T. B. W. Reid. 2 vols. A.N.T.S. IX–X, XII–XIII. Oxford, 1955, 1964.

Matzke   John E. Matzke, ed. *Les Œuvres de Simund de Freine.* Paris, 1909.

Pope   Mildred K. Pope. *From Latin to Modern French with Especial Consideration of Anglo-Norman: Phonology and Morphology.* 2nd edn., rev. Manchester, 1966.

Schlyter   Beneit. *La Vie de Thomas Becket par Beneit*, ed. Börje Schlyter. Lund, 1941.

Södergård   Östen Södergård, ed. *La Vie d'Édouard le Confesseur.* Uppsala, 1948.

T.-L.   A. Tobler – E. Lommatzsch. *Altfranzösisches Wörterbuch.* Berlin–Wiesbaden, 1915 ff.

Trethewey   William H. Trethewey, ed. *La Petite Philosophie.* A.N.T.S. I. Oxford, 1939.

PREFACE

When Werner Söderhjelm published *De saint Laurent* in 1888, he believed the copy of the poem found in the Paris MS., Bibliothèque nationale MS. fr. 19525, to be unique.[1] Just one year later, however, Paul Meyer reported on a manuscript recently acquired by the British Museum, Egerton 2710, in which there was another copy of the Anglo-Norman *Vie de St. Laurent*.[2] Five years after the publication of *De saint Laurent*, Söderhjelm published an article containing the variants from the Egerton MS. copy of the poem, and at the same time replied to some of the criticisms made by the distinguished reviewers of his edition.[3] However, in addition to the problem caused by the fact that the published text was based on only one MS., the edition had only a few critical notes, and lacked a detailed study of the language and a glossary. In short, Söderhjelm's *De saint Laurent* was not really a critical edition. The present edition has been undertaken to provide a critical text based on both the extant MSS. copies of the *St. Laurent*, accompanied by more extensive critical notes, an analysis of the language of the poem, and a glossary.

In the preparation of the edition I have received much help from Professors Peter Dembowski, John Flinn and Brian Merrilees, to whom go my thanks. I am also especially indebted to Professor A. R. Harden, at whose instigation I began my work on *St. Laurent*, and who gave generously of his time, erudition, and encouragement during his supervision of my doctoral dissertation at Toronto. And finally, my sincere thanks to Professor

---

[1] Werner Söderhjelm, *De saint Laurent, poème anglo-normand du XIIe siècle, publié pour la première fois d'après le manuscrit unique de Paris* (Paris, 1888).

[2] See 'Notice du ms. Egerton 2710 du Musée Britannique', *Bulletin de la Société des Anciens Textes Français*, 1889, 2^{e}p., 72–97.

[3] 'Le Poème de saint Laurent dans le ms. Egerton 2710 du Musée Britannique', *Mémoires de la Société Néophilologique de Helsingfors* I (1893), 21–31. The reviews were: G. Paris, *Romania* XVII (1888), 610–12; H. Suchier, *Literaturblatt für germanische und romanische Philologie* X (1888), 452–54; M. Wilmotte, *Le Moyen Âge* II (1889), 5–6.

T. B. W. Reid for his patient and expert guidance during the preparation of this edition. Publication has been assisted by a generous grant from the British Academy.

INTRODUCTION

THE MANUSCRIPTS

La Vie de St. Laurent is extant in two manuscripts, both written in England.

A. Paris, Bibliothèque Nationale, MS. fr. 19525.[1] The *Vie de St. Laurent* is the first item in this parchment manuscript which has 204 folios, measuring 225 by 155 mm., and which dates from the end of the thirteenth century. It is written in two meticulous hands, changing to the second hand at folio 67^r. *La Vie de St. Laurent* is written in two columns per page, with 32 lines per column. Sections of the poem are indicated by large capital initial letters, alternately red and blue; the first initial in the text, in blue and red, is the only one that is ornamented. The scribe has used few abbreviations and all are readily verifiable from the same or similar words written in full. Although a wrinkle in the manuscript distorts the microfilm copy of folio 2 recto and verso, a clear reading can be made from the manuscript itself.

As well as the *Vie de St. Laurent*, the manuscript includes a number of well-known Old French works. The contents of the manuscript are as follows.[2]

2. fo. 8^r *L'Assomption Nostre Dame*, from the *Bible* of Herman of Valenciennes.[3]

3. fo. 12^v *The Vision of St. Paul.*[4]

---

[1] This manuscript is described in detail by Ernst Martin in his introduction to *Le Besant de Dieu* (Halle, 1869); further details are given by Robert Reinsch in the introduction to his edition of 'Les Joies Nostre Dame', *Zeitschrift für romanische Philologie* III (1879), 200 ff., and by Henri Omont, *Catalogue des manuscrits français de la Bibliothèque nationale* (Paris, 1900), III, 339 ff.

[2] The numbering of the items in the manuscript has been added at a date later than that of the manuscript, and is not strictly followed in this enumeration.

[3] See *Romania* XV (1886), 308 for a list of other extant manuscript copies.

[4] Ed. L. E. Kastner, *Zeitschrift für französiche Sprache und Literatur* XXIX (1906), 274–90.

4. fo. 15^r *Vie de Sainte Marie l'Egyptienne.*[5]
5. fo. 26^v *La Vie de St. Alexis.*[6]
6–9. fos. 31^r–41^r A series of prose legends of John the Evangelist (fo. 31^r), John the Baptist (fo. 36^r), St. Bartholomew (fo. 38^v), SS. Peter (fo. 41^r) and Paul (fo. 42^r).[7]
10. fo. 43^v *Li Ver del juïse.*[8]
11. fo. 47^r *Grant mal fist Adam.*[9]
12. fo. 50^v *L'Évangile de Nicodème.*[10]
13. fo. 61^v An incomplete version of the *Sermon* of Guischart de Beauliu.[11]

One column and a half of folio 66^v are left blank; the second hand begins on folio 67^r and this section of the manuscript has some illuminations as well as coloured capital letters.

14. fo. 67^r *La Vie de Madeleine* by Guillaume le Clerc of Normandy.[12]
15. fo. 72^v A prose *Exposition on the Pater Noster* by Adam of Exeter.[13]
16. fo. 82^v A prose treatise on confession.[14]
17–20. A series of works by Guillaume le Clerc of Normandy: fo. 86^v *Les Joies Nostre Dame;*[15] fo. 96^r *Le*

---

[5] Ed. A. T. Baker, *Revue des langues romanes* LIX (1916–17), 145–401, printing in parallel columns Oxford MS. Corpus Christi 232, and a critical text based on all the other manuscripts.

[6] Early edns. by C. Hofmann (Munich, 1868) and G. Paris, L. Pannier (Paris, 1872).

[7] These prose legends are extant in this version in only four manuscripts, and nearly always as a group. Paris MS. Arsenal 3516 and B.N. fr. 19525 have all five legends, British Library MS. Harley 2253 lacks the legend of St. Paul, Egerton 2710 lacks those of John the Baptist and St. Paul. Paul Meyer has suggested that these legends together with the version of the Gospel of Nicodemus found in these latter three manuscripts, formed an early small legendary. See *Histoire littéraire de la France* XXXIII (Paris, 1906), 393 ff.

[8] Ed. H. von Feilitzen (Uppsala, 1883).

[9] The latest edition is by W. Suchier, *Zwei altfranzösiche Reimpredigten* (Halle, 1949).

[10] Ed. Alvin E. Ford (Geneva, 1973).

[11] Ed. A. Gabrielson (Uppsala and Leipzig, 1909).

[12] Ed. Robert Reinsch, *Archiv für das Studium der neueren Sprachen und Literaturen* LXIV (1880), 85–94.

[13] See M. Dominica Legge, *Anglo-Norman Literature and its Background* (Oxford, 1963), pp. 226–27.

[14] Brief extracts of this work extant in other copies are published in *Archiv* LXIII (1880), 64, and *Romania* XXXII (1903), 95.

[15] Ed. R. Reinsch, *Z. r. Ph.* III (1879), 200–25.

Besant de Dieu;[16] fo. 125^r *Les Treiz Moz;*[17] fo. 129^r *La Vie de Tobie.*[18] Folio 132^r has only twelve lines; fo. 132^v is blank. Folios 123–132 have blank spaces for large capital initial letters which have not been supplied.

21. fo. 141^v *Vie de Sainte Marguerite.*[19]
22. fo. 145^r *Le Roman des romans.*[20]
23. fo. 153^r A series of five sermons in Latin and French, based on the Bible: (a) fo. 153^r; (b) fo. 170^r; (c) fo. 174^r; (d) fo. 180^r; (e) fo. 184^v.[21]
24. fos. 191^v–202^v A version of the Passion from the *Bible* of Herman of Valenciennes, also found in Egerton 2710 and Harley 2253. Folio 203 is blank; fo. 204^r has a fragment of a song, in a new hand, with musical notation: *Margot, Margot, grief sunt ly mau damer.*

B. London, British Library, Egerton 2710.[22] *La Vie de St. Laurent* is the last item in this vellum manuscript which has 151 folios, measuring 265 by 180 mm., which are usually written in two columns of 40 or 42 lines per page. The large initial letters are alternately red and blue, occasionally gold. The manuscript is dated (by Meyer and the British Museum *Catalogue*) in the last half of the thirteenth century. There is a full-page ink drawing on folio 1, col. b, 'of Our Lord seated on an altar supported by two angels' (*Catalogue*, p. 458), and a similar drawing in the margin of folio 35, col. b, dating from the fourteenth century.

---

[16] Ed. Ernst Martin (Halle, 1869); ed. Pierre Ruelle (Brussels, 1973).

[17] Ed. R. Reinsch, *Z. r. Ph.* III (1879), 225–231.

[18] Ed. R. Reinsch, *Archiv* LXII (1879), 375–96; see also Ruth J. Dean, 'A Missing Chapter in the *Vie de Tobie*', *Modern Philology* XXXIII (1935–36), 13–19.

[19] Ed. A. Scheler (Antwerp, 1877); ed. A. Joly (Paris, 1879). See also *Wace. La Vie de Sainte Marguerite*, ed. Elizabeth A. Francis (Paris, 1932), pp. vii–xiii for a brief description of the different extant versions. The version in our MS. *A* is not that of Wace (as Joly believed), nor is it the Fouque version as noted in R. Bossuat, *Manuel Bibliographique* (Melun, 1951), number 3425.

[20] Ed. F. J. Tanquerey, *Deux poèmes moraux anglo-français: Le Roman des romans et Le Sermon en vers* (Paris, 1922).

[21] See *Romania* XXXII (1903), 106 for extracts of these sermons from other extant copies.

[22] For detailed descriptions see Paul Meyer, 'Notice du ms. Egerton 2710 du Musée Britannique', *Bulletin de la Société des Anciens Textes Français* (1889), 72–97, and the *Catalogue of Additions to the Manuscripts in the British Museum 1883–1893* (London, 1894), pp. 457–8.

A marginal note at the bottom of folio 83, col. b, indicates that the manuscript belonged to the nuns of Derby Priory at the end of the fifteenth century. The contents of MS. *B* are as follows:

1. fo. 1[r] An Anglo-Norman poem based on the Old Testament.[2 3]
2. fo. 112[r] The Passion from the *Bible* of Herman of Valenciennes, cf. item 24, above.
3. fo. 126[r] *L'Évangile de Nicodème*, cf. item 12, above.
4. fo. 134[r] *Grant mal fist Adam*, cf. item 11, above.
5. fo. 136[r] *L'Assomption Nostre Dame*, cf. item 2, above.
6–8. The prose legends of John the Evangelist (fo. 139[r]), St. Peter (fo. 142[v]), St. Bartholomew (fo. 143[v]); cf. items 6–9, above.
9. fo. 145[r] The *Sermon* of Guischart de Beauliu, cf. item 13, above.
10. fo. 148[v] *La Vie de Seint Laurent*. As opposed to the previous items in verse in this manuscript, this poem is written as prose with a dot regularly separating the lines, except for ll. 228–229, 280–81, and the section at ll. 442–47, where the divisions are made erratically within the line. The pages are in two columns of 44 lines each. The same divisions in the poem as found in the MS. *A* version are made here, by means of large ornamented initial letters, which are alternately red and blue. The poem is preceded by a two-line rubric, as are items 4, 7, and 8 in this manuscript. The scribe used many abbreviations, discussed below. The space left after *St. Laurent* in the last column of fo. 151[v] is filled with an incomplete exposition in French on the seven petitions in the Pater Noster (written in Latin). The fragment ends during the treatment of the first petition.

Comparison of the Manuscripts

Paul Meyer mentioned the close relationship that exists between

---

[2 3] There are six extant manuscript copies, published in excerpts. See P. Meyer, *BSATF* (1889), 73 ff. and *Notices et Extraits* XXXIV, i, 210–11; F. Bonnardot, *Romania* XVI (1887), 177–213; J. Bonnard, *Traductions de la Bible en vers* (Paris, 1884), pp. 92 ff.

the two manuscripts containing the *Vie de St. Laurent* in his
'Notice du ms. Egerton 2710 du Musée Britannique' in 1889,
pointing out that five of the ten items in Egerton 2710 were
also in B.N. MS. fr. 19525. At this time Meyer was unaware that
in fact all but the first item (and the final fragment) of our MS.
B was also in our MS. *A*. Later, however, in an article on
hagiographical legends in prose he drew attention to the com-
mon contents of our two manuscripts during his description of
a small legendary extant in only four manuscripts (two of which
were our MSS. *A* and *B*).[24]

Yet despite the close connection between the contents of
these two manuscripts (especially between the section of MS. *A*
written by the first scribe, and MS. *B*, items 2–10), there is no
indication given by a comparison of the two versions of the *St.
Laurent* that one scribe was copying from the other. Rather, it
is probable that both versions were copied from a common
source, since both have recorded the same details of the legend
in the same sequence and metre, including even the same ambi-
guous passages. Take, for example, the passage beginning at l.
439, where the saint, to the infinite bewilderment of Decius,
puns on the difference between things created by God and
those created by man. Both manuscripts appear to have a line
missing in the midst of this discussion, at ll. 450–51, and
neither scribe has attempted to edit or elucidate the passage.
Similarly, both manuscripts appear to have a line or lines mis-
sing at 899–900.

At some points in the text MS. *B* is superior to MS. *A*; for
example, at ll. 34, 35, 43, 142, 164, 176, 403, 440, 481, 942,
and perhaps at ll. 550, 820.

More frequently, however, MS. *A* gives a better reading than
B, as at ll. 23, 85, 89–90, 101, 139, 199, 205, 210–11 (the
scribe of *B* leaps from one word to its repetition a line later),
246, 254, 257, 282, 292, 310, 407, 538, 585, 864. As well, the
scribe of *B* makes occasional slips, such as the expansion of l.
363 into two lines, or the reduction of ll. 779–80 to one line,
or the omission of ll. 578–79.

It would seem, then, that neither manuscript version is a

---

[24] See above, MS. *A*, items 6–9, and note.

direct copy of the other. Rather, the similarity of the two ver-
sions suggests that both were copied from the same source, now
unknown, which in turn was a copy of a hypothetical origi-
nal.[25]

The choice of MS. *A* as the base manuscript for this edition
has been made on the grounds that MS. *A* is more frequently
superior to *B* than *B* is to *A*.

LANGUAGE

I. Phonology

An analysis of the words found in rhyme in *St. Laurent* reveals
the following features of the language of the poem.

1. [e] from Latin tonic free *a* rhymes only with itself; as is
usual, the vowel is [e] and not [ie] in *regné* < *regnatum* 512 (:
trinité). The scribes of both manuscripts frequently reduce *-ie*
to *-e* in spelling.

2. [er] from Latin tonic free *a* + *r* is found: (a) once in
rhyme with [er], the reduced form of [ier] derived from Latin
tonic *a* free preceded by a palatal followed by *r*: *delaisser* < *de*
+ *laxare* 549 (: *aorer*), and (b) once in rhyme with [er], the
reduced form of [ier] from the Latin ending *-eriu*: *mester* <
ministerium 7 (: *esprover*).

3. The Old French diphthongs [ai] and [ei] rhyme when
followed by a nasal: *ovraigne* 67 (: *peine*), *saint* 323 (: *ensaint*)

---

[25] The same conclusion was reached by W. Söderhjelm in his article on the
variants from MS. *B*, in *Mémoires de la Société Néophilologique de Helsingfors* I
(1893), 21–31. The author's haste in dealing with the variants from MS. *B* can be
seen in internal discrepancies in his study, which must also be faulted for misreadings
of the manuscript (Söderhjelm was working from a copy supplied by a second
person). Examples of discrepancies found between his initial complete list of variants
and a second short list of better readings from *B* are the following: l. 171, and *image*
211, appear only in the second list; *dit* 230 becomes *dist* in the second list, and
similarly *guerpis errur e seu* 594 becomes *guerpis tesrour e siu*. Examples of misread-
ings, found in the initial list of variants, are: *enciltre* for *encuntre* 200, *delaisser* for
lesser 549, *vint* for *unt* 576. Occasionally, as well, similar mistakes occur in Söder-
hjelm's edition of MS. *A*. Examples of misprints or misreadings are the following:
dreiciez for *dreciez* 1, *ceo qui homme . . . qui est fait* for *ceo que homme . . . quis fait*
441, *ou* for *que* 657, *aveent* for *aveient* 887, etc. (similar slips are made at ll. 94, 234,
303, 330, 390, 419, 486, 507, 514, 540, 569, 576, 595, 596, 609, 636, 655, 656,
657, 682, 737, 785, 812, 883, 912, 914).

etc.; this rhyme is noted as early as the *St. Brendan*. There appear to have been no rhymes between [ai] and [ei] in final position in the original of *St. Laurent*, although MS. *B* does have one variant reading which uses this rhyme: *lei* < *legem* 594 (: *fai*, imper. 2). The reading in MS. *A* (*lei* imper. 2 of *laier*, rhyming with *fai*) is probably that of the original (although the sense is repetitive), since this is the only example in the text of a possible rhyme between [ai] and [ei] in final position.

There is one rhyme which shows the reduction of [ai] to [ε]: *les* < *laxo* 202 (: *aprés*); there are no examples of the phonetic reduction of [ei] to a simple sound.[26]

4. [ãn] and [ẽn] do not rhyme, except for *serjant* 231, 272 (: *avant*), 249 (: *mescreant*), 520 (: *tirant*), and *maltalant* 517 (: *entent*). Both these words are among the recognized exceptions to the usually rigorously separated [ãn]/[ẽn] Anglo-Norman rhymes.[27]

5. The product of Vulgar Latin close *o* free rhymes with that of Vulgar Latin close *o* checked: *jor* 411 (: *enpereor*), 748 (: *honor*), 912 (: *douçor*).

6. The hypothetical triphthong derived from *focum* is reduced to a single sound: *fu* 871, 883 (: *entendu*), 875 (: *fu* < *fuit*); the words derived from *jocum* and *locum* are found only in rhyme together: *leus* 762 : *gieus*.

7. The product of Latin *ū* + yod rhymes with the product of Latin *ŭ* + yod: *fruiz* < *frūctum* 494 (: *cruiz* < *crŭcem*). The isolated rhyme *lui* 570 (: *Tyberii*) suggests that the diphthong is ascending.

8. *c* is used to represent the evolution of *p* + yod intervocalic in *sace* < *sapiat* 699 (: *grace*). Latin *c* before *a* usually is written *ch* by the scribes: *char* 503, *charbun* 841; but *c* or *k* is retained in *Capitoile* 244, *catasta* 691, *kalende* 746.

9. The vocalization of preconsonantal *l* after *a* is not proven by examples in rhyme, although the spelling frequently suggests it: *haut* 417 (: *faut*), etc.

10. Final [m] and [n] are not distinguished in rhyme: *araim* 435 (: *vain*), *non* < *nomen* 95 (: *region*), 707 (: *oroison*). Final

---

[26] For a discussion of the development of these rhymes see Pope § 1157; Trethewey, pp. xxix–xxxi, xlviii–l; Matzke, pp. xxiv–xxvi; Schlyter, pp. 42 ff.

[27] See H. Suchier, *Reimpredigt* (Halle, 1879), pp. 69–71.

[n] has fallen in rhyme after [r] : *jor* 411 (: *enpereor*), 748 (: *honor*), 912 (: *douçor*). Palatalized [ñ] rhymes with unpalatalized [n] : *ovraigne* 67 (: *peine*), 456 (: *semaine*).

11. In *laies* 673 (: *plaies*) the fem. form has been modified by analogy with the masc. form, where, under the influence of S.-W. Old French, the final dental of *lait* fell (cf. Pope §1197).

II. Orthography

Orthography of MS. A

In the spelling of O.F. [ai] MS. *A* often retains *ai*, but also uses *ei* (*sei* 21, 278), and *e* (*les* 202, *mes* 69). Conversely, *ai* represents O.F. [ɛ] occasionally (*maitre* 569, 635). For Western O.F. [ei] the spellings *ei* and *ai* (*estait* 273, *mains* 18, *paine* 472, *vaie* 53, etc.), or *oi* (*croire* 291, 293, *moi* 140, *soit* 297, etc.) are found frequently; the diphthong is once represented by *ie* (*estriene* 473). O.F. [ie] is often reduced to *e* in spelling in rhyme-words (*apareiller* 361: *seigner*, *chevaler* 767: *drecier*, *despoiller* 518: *aiglenter*, *despoillez* 665: *iriez*, *escumengé* 558: *renoié*, *evesche* 108: *clergié*, *mesnee* 371: *baptisee*, 391: *apareillee*, etc.) and within the line (*chef* 101, *chevaler* 216, etc.). O.F. [ue] is generally spelled *ue* (*puet* 8, 17, etc., *muert* 51, etc.), occasionally *o* (*iloc* 237, 720, 742, 909, etc., *poples* 699), once *oi* (*coivre* 14). O.F. [ui] can be spelled *oi* (*poisse* 813: *angoisse*). O.F. [u] from Latin ō and ŭ is usually spelled *o* or *ou* in MS. *A*, as opposed to *u* in MS. *B* (*amor* 63, 747, etc., *amour* 65, etc. /amur*; *tormenz* 61, etc. / *turmenz*; *tristor* 770, etc. / *tristur*).

The scribe of *A* replaces effaced consonants only rarely (*baptesme* 374, *baptisee* 372, etc., as opposed to *Averser* 475, *aversitez* 10, *chaitis* 534, *granment* 600, etc.). Final supported *d* sometimes replaces [t] (*mund* 465: *respont*, 647, etc.). Preconsonantal *l* is often written *u* (*ceus* 92, *haut* 417: *faut, maus* 687, *vaut* 43, etc.), although *l* is occasionally retained in spelling (*bealté* 42, *salter* 154, 458, etc. In *B*, *l* is frequently kept in spelling). O.F. [s] can be spelled *z* in final position (*muablez* 25: *parmanablez*), and *c* in initial position (*ciecle* 702, etc.).

Orthography of MS. B

In the spelling system of *B*, O.F. [ai] can be written *ai, ei,* or *e* (*cheitifs* 693, *eit* 56: *fet, fere* 82: *retrere, leis* 202, *pleisir* 315, *vet* 303, etc.). O.F. [ei] is limited in spelling to *ei* and *e* (*aver* 33, *crere* 293, *decrestre* 419, etc.). Derivatives of Latin words in *-ationem* are spelled *-eisun* (*oreisun* 706, *reisun* 449, as opposed to *oroisun* and *raisun* in *A*). The reduction of O.F. [ie] to *e* in spelling is more frequent in *B* than in *A* (additional examples are *clergé* 107, *drecez* 1, *sé* 576, *trencher* 207: *chevaler*, etc.). The O.F. diphthong [ue] is spelled *o* (*pople* 699, *pot* 8, 17, etc., *orgoil* 346, *iloc* 720, etc.), and *eu* (*ileuc* 237, 353, 404, etc.). O.F. [yi] is often reduced in spelling to *u* (*fruz* 494: *croiz, destrure* 100, 105, *relust* 825); once [y] is spelled *ui* (*reconuit* 229: *ut*).

More frequently in *B* than in *A* the spelling of countertonic vowels reflects the modification of these sounds in the language of the scribe: *chescun* 27, 547 is the usual A.-N. form, as opposed to *A*'s *chascun; assait* 269 (*A: essait*, although both manuscripts have the countertonic vowel changed before [r] in *sarmone* 109, *sarmoner* 335); *bosoing* 9, 13, etc. (*A: besoing*); *esponter* 788 (*A: espoenter*); *pour* 180, 566, 604 (as opposed to *A: poor* 180, *peour* 566, 604); *provost* 267, etc. (*A: prevost*). In other instances vowels in hiatus have been effaced: *age* 198 (*A: aage*), *esleça* 259 (*A: esleeça*), *juneisons* 934 (*A: jeunesons*), *maluré* 880 (*A: maleuré*).

The spelling of [ñ] varies in *B*: intervocalically it is written *ign* (*overaigne* 67, 456) as in *A*, or *ing* (*overainge* 57: *parmainge*), or *n* (*primsené* 733). In final position it is written *ing* (*bosoing* 9, etc.), or *n* (*engin* 71, 798) as in *A*, or *ig* (*bosuig* 15; cf. *Horn* II, p. 74).

O.F. [s] is retained before unvoiced consonants in both manuscripts (*beneistre / benestre* 362, *chascuns / chescun* 27, *creistra / crestra* 419, etc.). In *B* alone O.F. [z] is sometimes effaced before a voiced consonant (*deverie* 881, *devez* 421, 844, *hidur* 887, *hidus* 792 — although *mesdire* 17, *mesdit* 16 are also found). In rhymes, the scribe of *B* seems to have considered *s* before *t* to be silent (*Crist* 363: *dit, dist* 894: *vit, dust* 143: *sut, fist* 463: *dit, vist* 142: *dit*). The spelling *sc* is used in endings

-esce (*pruesce* 36: *richesce*, etc.), and in *prophescie* 146. Three spellings are found for *ici* 135 / *isci* 20 / *issi* 116.

Learned influence, seen in the spelling *ph* in *prophetiza* 155, *prophete* 852, etc. of both manuscripts, is stronger in *B*, where previously effaced consonants are replaced in such words as *adversitez* 10, *adverser* 475, *grantment* 600 (and *baptisee* 372 etc., as in *A*) and double consonants are used (*accusez* 864, *afflicciuns* 935, *barres* 837, etc.). Within the line the scribe of *B* is inclined to retain the consonants *f, l,* and *p* before a flexional *s* (*chaitifs* 534, *nuls* 201, *colps* 617). Final supported *d* replaces [t] more often than in *A*: additional examples are *rend* 302, 830, *surd* 434. The consistent use of *d* in *ad* < *habet* and *od* < *apud* may be diacritical in *B*.

In the treatment of learned loan-words, MS. *B* reveals more archaic features than *A*, e.g. in *vigilies* 935 (*A: vegiles*), *virgine* 477 (*A: virge*). The unfamiliar consonant group resulting from the slurring of the penultimate vowel has been reformed in *alme* 906, but not in *apostles* 348 (*A: apostres*), *deacne* 122, *deakne* 245 (*A: diacre*), *archidecne* 246 (*A* also has *archidiacnes* 128, 246, and *diacnes* 127), nor in *virgne* 481, 482, 483 (*A: virge*). The archaic forms *estorie* 77, etc., *glorie* 26, etc., *gramarie* 804, *memorie* 78, etc., *vicarie* 273, and *victorie* 624, etc. persist in *B* (except for *estoire* 805, *apostoille* 86, 243), as opposed to the forms *estoire, gloire*, etc. in *A*. Somewhat similarly *B* has *martirie* 64 (*martire* in *A*); but both manuscripts have *(re)fri-gerie* 862, 872, 885, *miserie* 863, also *obsequie* 755.

Conclusion

The study of the spelling of both manuscripts reveals characteristics which are of a later date than the phonetic traits found in the study of the rhyme-words. MS. *A* shows a wide range of interchangeable graphies for O.F. [ai], [ei], and [ɛ], which suggests that [ai] and [ei] have levelled to [ɛ], a phonetic feature of thirteenth-century Anglo-Norman. The most persistent thirteenth-century trait is the use of the digraph *oi* for Western O.F. [ei], a feature common in Central O.F. The replacement of supported final [t] by *d* is also a thirteenth-century feature found in *A*.

The thirteenth-century spelling traits found in MS. *B* include the interchangeable graphies for [ai] and [ei], although they are more limited than in *A*, the most common being *e*; the replacement of final supported [t] by *d*; and the use of the digraph *sc* for [s] < [ts]. In contrast to these thirteenth-century characteristics, MS. *B* incorporates archaic spellings of certain learned loan-words, not found in *A*.

It seems evident, then, that both manuscripts are thirteenth-century copies of the poem, and that *B* presents a more archaic version than does *A*.

III. Morphology

A. Gender

The gender of nouns as indicated by articles, attributive adjectives, and pronouns is always that of standard O.F. *Miracles* 322 (masc.), 334 (fem.) and *umbre* 22 (masc.) could have either gender in O.F.

Among adjectives derived from Latin two-termination adjectives, *grant* 214, 268, 392, and *tel* 314n, 946n, are found without analogical *-e*, as opposed to *brieve* 25. The adjectives *commun, dolz* and *fol*, as is normal in O.F., are treated as belonging to the *bon/bone* type (cf. ll. 60, 572; 555, 557; 212, 549).

B. Declension

The rhymes between traditionally inflected forms and forms which are not morphologically regular, such as masc. nom. sg. *dolenz* 649: *tormenz* masc. nom. pl., masc. nom. sg. *iriez* 664: *despoillez* masc. acc. sg., nom. sg. *rei* 640: *mei*, etc., suggest that the declension system was breaking down for the author of *St. Laurent*, and the confusion in declension cannot be attributed only to the scribe.

In the masc. nom. sg. of parisyllabic nouns and adjectives found in rhyme, the traditionally inflected forms are almost twice as frequent as forms without *-s* (*-z*). If all instances within the line and in rhyme are considered, however, the ratio of

forms with final -*s* (-*z*) to forms without the inflexion is almost
1:1. Only in the declension of the word *fiz/fil* does the tradi-
tionally nom. sg. form function as acc. sg. (ll. 133, 480, as
opposed to *fil* 481).

The traditional forms in the nom. pl. of masc. parisyllabic
nouns and adjectives are more frequently found than forms
with -*s* (-*z*). In rhyme, the traditional form is always found,
except for *tormenz* 648 (: *dolenz* nom. sg.). When all the forms
within the line and in rhyme are considered, the ratio of the
traditional forms to the forms with -*s* (-*z*) is about 5:1.

There are isolated instances of an analogical -*s* in the nom. sg.
of *Peres* 646, rhyming with the similarly modified *Salveres*, and
within l. 365, and *Crieres* 468. Except for this analogical -*s* in
Salveres and *Crieres*, and the scribal use of *homme* 441, 443,
445 as nom. sg. (see Notes), the imparisyllabic nouns found in
the poem are used with the traditional forms.

The past participles of verbs conjugated with *estre* sometimes
lack the usual inflexions to show agreement with the subject: in
rhyme, the masc. nom. sg. is found without -*s* (-*z*) at ll. 6, 38,
279, 382, 388, 547, 579, 769, and within the line at ll. 163,
164, 313, 836, 864. The masc. nom. pl. has -*s* (-*z*) at ll. 322 (in
rhyme) and 568. As is usual in O.F., there are instances where
no agreement is made where the subject follows, or the parti-
ciple precedes the conjugated verb (e.g. ll. 247, 642, 725, 751,
835).

Past participles of verbs conjugated with *aveir* occasionally
show agreement with a preceding direct object (e.g. ll. 223, 372,
827 in rhyme, and within the line at 222, 230). The masc. acc.
sg. is once found in rhyme with -*z*, l. 665. More frequently,
however, the past participle is invariable (cf. ll. 146, 151, 285,
407, 416, 654, 733, etc.).

As well as the invariable forms of proper names, such as
Sixte, Ypolite, etc., Latin forms are often used in the nom., e.g.
Sixtus, Ypolitus, Justinus, etc. In some names, used infrequent-
ly in the text, the Latin nom. form is generalized, e.g. *Agapitus,
Feliscissimus, Lucillus, Romanus*. In the more frequently used
Jesus/Jesu, the form *Jesus* (*Deus*) is usually nom. (once acc., l.
663), the form *Jesu* is usually acc. (once nom., l. 949), and the
form *Jesu Crist* is almost equally nom. (ll. 298, 302, 308, 467)

and acc. (ll. 326, 363, 710, 731, 869). Similarly, *Deu* (*Damnedeu*) is both nom. (ll. 83, 295, 313, 344, 675, 696, etc.) and acc. (ll. 62, 65, 113, 120, etc.); the form *Dé* is always acc. (ll. 161, 740); *Deus* (ll. 38, 345, 348, etc.) is always nominative.

The name of the martyr, *Lorenz*, is subject to no variation in the text. The title-adjective *saint* is also invariable (except for *sain* 878); when this word is used as a noun, it is found in the nom. once as *sains* 904, and once as *saint* 695. The title word *danz/dan*, declined traditionally, is found only twice, ll. 40, 155.

The name of the tyrant is consistently used with Latin flexional endings. The nominative is always *Decius* (*Cesar*), ll. 95, 117, 130, 170, etc. The possessive genitive forms *Cesaris* and *Decii* are found at ll. 216, 387, 888. *Decio*, the dative form, appears in ll. 258, 403, 895. The accusative *Decium* is found after prepositions of motion or place (ll. 247, 838), and after *a* to express the indirect object (ll. 533, 860). The ablative *Decio* is used once in an absolute construction, l. 422.

Latin flexional endings are also frequently used in the possessive genitive with other names, e.g. *temple Jovis* 760, *temple Martis* 205, etc., *termes Olimpiadis* 761, *paleis Tyberii* 571, 910, *le grant sen Aristotilis* 39, *la richeise dan Cesaris* 40, and *la quart ide augusti* 933 (as opposed to *le theatre Auguste* 764, *le palais Saluste* 765).

Jeo serves as both the strong and weak form in the nom. of the first person sg. personal pronoun (e.g. strong at l. 795, weak at ll. 197, 236, 252, 514, 515, etc.). The strong acc. form in the first pers. sg. is once *mi*, l. 709, in rhyme, as opposed to the usual *mei* or *moi*. The weak indirect object *te* is allowed to begin the line at 402, 597, 599. *Te* is also once used in the nom. sg., l. 507 (*B* has *tu*). In the third pers. sg. the form *lui* is used indiscriminately for both the strong masc. (ll. 7, 66, 78, 234, 388, 390, 391, etc.) and the indirect weak masc. pronoun object (ll. 162, 270, 290, 324, 325, 327, etc.). The weak form *li* occurs but rarely in the text, e.g. ll. 827, 914. The scribal form *lei* 231, 275, 523, 724 (with infin.), 741, 857, is used for the masc. direct object, always after the verb (the corresponding form in *B* is *le* 231, 275, 724, 741, and missing, 523, 857).

Except for scribal *se* 77 (fem. sg.), the standard Western

French forms are used for the weak possessive adjectives, although *ton* functions as nom. (ll. 444, 586, 596) as well as acc. As is usual in O.F., the vowel of the feminine singular forms is elided, ll. 63, 65, 209, 309, 702, 802, etc. The tonic forms of the possessive adjectives are used with the definite article (e.g. *le mien Pere* 815, and at ll. 137, 710), and with the indefinite article (e.g. *un suen serjant* 272).

The nom. form of the relative pronoun is normally *qui* (*ki*), but occasionally *que*, e.g. ll. 23, 234, 817. In all functions of *que* the scribe frequently writes the full form where the original must have had an elided form, e.g. ll. 234, 316, 379, 416, 441, 443, 445, etc. In its absolute function *qui* (*ki*) is often used in the sense of 'he who', e.g. ll. 48, 49, 80, etc.; it appears in the conditional sense of 'if one' in l. 103 and in the possessive sense of 'whose' (for *cui*) in l. 514.

In addition to their traditional accusative sg. function elsewhere in the text, *cel* and *(i)cest* serve as nom. sg. at ll. 498, 500, 502, 503, as opposed to the traditional forms *cil* and *(i)cist* at ll. 495, 504, etc.; MS. *A* has *cil* as acc. sg. in l. 605 (*lui* in *B*). The forms with analogical *i-* are found infrequently (about 1/7 of all occurrences). There are no forms with *-ui* or *-i*.

Indefinite pronouns found in the poem are declined traditionally, except for the nom. sg. *nul* found without *-s*, ll. 32, 33, 35, 201 (*nuls* in *B*), 342. The definite article may be used with the pronoun *en* (*om*), ll. 318, 451, 585, 692, or omitted, ll. 44, 182, 454. In the declension of *toz*, both the form *tot* (l. 471) and the traditional *tuit* are used for the masc. nom. pl. There is one instance of *toz* (adj.) functioning as the masc. nom. pl., l. 46, and once *tout*, l. 578, is masc. nom. sg.

The declension of the definite article shows a degree of simplification similar to that found in the masc. parisyllabic nouns and adjectives. In the masc. nom. sg. the form *le* is found almost as frequently as the traditional form *li* (e.g. ll. 4, 39, 41, 578, 695, 907 as opposed to ll. 21, 25, 51, 290, 494, 635, 834, 904). In one instance *li* functions as masc. acc. sg., l. 418 (rejected in the text). The traditional forms are consistently used for the plural definite article. The indefinite article in the masc. nom. sg. appears as *un* on one occasion, l. 692, as opposed to the traditional *uns*, ll. 707, 762, 835.

C. Conjugation

The only verb to show hesitancy in conjugation is *rostir* 889, which has *rostent* 843, ind. pr. 6.

In the singular endings of the present tenses, only the traditional forms without analogical *-e* are used in ind. pr. 1 and subj. pr. 3 of first-conj. verbs, e.g. ll. 19, 59, 75, 129, 196, 202, 324, 398, 433, 514, 551, 603, 605, 656. The Western French analogical endings occur a few times within the line, subj. pr. 2 *muerges* 189, subj. pr. 3 *vienge* 315, *sovienge* 3. The imperative of *prendre* uses the shortened radical, *pren* 187, metathesized in *pernez* 688. The first pers. pl. endings of the present tenses are always *-um, -un, -on*, e.g. *prium* 65, *lisum* 84, *trovun* 458, *trovon* 347. The ind. pr. 4 of *estre* is *summes* 172, *sunmes* 721. *Aler* has only *vait* 150, 303, etc. as the ind. pr. 3 form. The subj. pr. 3 of *doner* appears as *doinst* 67, 314, 941, 946, or *donst* 72.

There is one example of syllabic alternation in the radical; *manger* 561 has *manjue* 505 as ind. pr. 3. Vocalic alternation of radicals is frequent in the text, e.g. *amaint* 254 − *amené* 382; *ceile* 783 − *celez* 9; *muert* 51 − *morras* 176; *trueve* 32 − *trover* 149; *veut* 78 − *voleir* 43; etc. In *plore* 771 − *plorer* 772, the diphthong in the strong radical is reduced in spelling to *o*. In the verb *(de)preier* both radicals have the same vowel, *pri* 60, *prie* 730, *prient* 307 − *prié* 402, *prium* 65, *deprier* 240. The verb *otreier* appears only once, with *i* in the weak radical, *otrié* 401. The strong radical has replaced the weak radical in *remaindrez* 119; the weak radical is maintained, at least in spelling, in *devendrum* 124, *revendras* 508. The radical with infix *-is-* is used in *esjois* 773, and the palatalized radical in *oi* 785, *oiant* 417, 423.

In the future, the radical consonant has been assimilated in *dorai* 193; the radicals of *entrer* and *mostrer* remain unchanged, *entrerai* 903, *mostrera* 327. The *rr* has been reduced in spelling to *r* in *orez* 377, but kept in *morras* 176. The future of *aveir* occasionally has the northern forms *arai* 774, *ara* 83, as opposed to the usual *avra* 318, 328, *avras* 610, 630, *avrunt* 510, 511. The future of *estre* is dimorphic: *seras* 140, 428, *seron* 20, 138 and *iert* 6, 9, 352, 586, 612, 821; *iere* 554, *ieres* 547 are no

doubt scribal for *ier, iers* (see note). The stem of *fere* is always written *fer-*, as in *ferai* 134, 135, etc., *feras* 175, *ferun* 426, although it probably was at times *fr-* (see Versification).

The imperfect has the standard endings of Central French, the spelling being usually *-ei-* or *-oi-*, e.g. *esteient* 886, *estoient* 473, occasionally *-ai-*, *estait* 273. The imperfect of *estre* also appears as *ert* 96, 267, 277, 692, 929, *erent* 88, 792.

The preterite of *aveir*-type verbs has *ou* or *u* in the strong radical: *out* 90, 95, 268, etc., *ut* 230; *pout* 149, *sut* 144.

The past participle *beneit* 733 of *beneistre* is probably scribal for *beneeit* (see Versification, Number of Syllables), rhyming with *receit*, rather than *beneït*. The past participle of *chaeir* is *chaue* 214 (fem. sg.). There are two strong *s*-type past participles, *ars* 867, *ocis* 428.

IV. Syntax and Style

The following points of syntax and style are characteristic of *La Vie de St. Laurent*.

1. The juxtaposed oblique is used with the names of persons or of the divinity, with the value of the Latin possessive genitive, as in *la maisun / Ypolite* 409–10, *une ancele saint Lorenz* 76, *le cors saint Lorenz* 923, *por l'amor Dé* 161, *l'oes Deu* 164, *es membres Deu* 165, *as povres Deu* 223, *al feel Deu* 543, *merci Dé* 740, and the more archaic formula *por Deu amor* 714, and with *Jesu, la passiun Jesu* 492, *el nun Jesu* 715, 734, *el nun sun Seignor Jesu Crist* 731. (For the use of Latin inflexions for possessive genitive, see Morphology, B, above.) Possession may also be indicated by prepositions, either *de, l'estreine / De Adam et de Evam* 473–74, *membre de deable* 430, *voiz del deable* 682, or *a, engins al deable* 71, *menbre al deable* 158, *commandement al tirant* 521. The traditional use of the oblique in absolute constructions for adverbial expressions of manner, etc., is also found, e.g. *oiant trestoz* 417, *oiant toz* 423, *veant Decio* 422 (here the Latin ablative is retained).

2. The definite article is normally omitted with abstract nouns and nouns denoting unique objects or beings (*ciel et mer et terre rounde* 469, for example) but certain parallel

constructions demonstrate a varying usage of the definite article: *Vie est brieve, li mund muablez* 25; *Cel porta la mort en la pome / Et cest, vie en la char de homme* 502—3; *Qui mal unt fait, mal avrunt* 510, but *Le bien avrunt qui bien fait unt* 511.

The indefinite article is once used with collective force, *unes coroies* 'set of thongs, scourge' 668.

3. There is occasional confusion, as often in O.F., between the second persons sg. and pl., e.g. *Baptisez mei . . . el nun Jesu tun Creator / Qui te deigna revisiter* 714—16. Though *tote gent* 440 takes a singular verb, *gent* qualified by other adjectives has a plural verb in ll. 633, 826, 937; somewhat similarly *Nel voloit justise desfaire, / Ne il ne l'ossent lesser aler* 282—3. For ll. 260—61 see the note.

4. There is one example of a reflexive verb conjugated with *aveir, Mei ai en sacrefise osfert* 847.

5. The gerund is used in absolute constructions (see 1, above), and as a complement of the preposition *en* in l. 695. The present participle is used adjectivally in ll. 524, 636, 671, 841. Although common in other Anglo-Norman texts, there are no instances in *St. Laurent* of the verbal periphrasis which uses *aler* (and similar verbs of motion) + gerund or *estre* + present participle (cf. *Horn* II, 89—90).

6. The infinitive negated by *ne* serves as a second person sg. imperative, ll. 584, 596, 772, and perhaps originally in l. 190n. There is one instance of the jussive infinitive, *Or del sofrir* 782.

As complement of a verb, the simple infinitive is used with *quider* 100, and *doner* ('grant') 67, 314, as well as with other verbs normally found with this construction in O.F., such as *oir* 93—94, 252, *oser* 283, *deigner* 299, etc. The infinitive preceded by *a*, as is usual in O.F., is complement of verbs such as *covenir* 335, *estre* (+ adj.) 792—93, *aveir* (+ noun) 251, 320. With *commander* the simple infinitive is a complement once, l. 537; more usually the infinitive complement is preceded by *a*, 207, 518, except when the indirect object of *commander* is itself preceded by *a*, ll. 204—5, 723—24.

The preposition *por* preceding the infinitive is frequently

used to express purpose, e.g. ll. 97, 475, 572, etc. Once the infinitive is introduced by *a* after the comparative conjunction *k'*, l. 18.

7. *Voleir* + infinitive is used with reduced force, equivalent to 'choose to, think fit to' in ll. 282, 530, 548, and signifying 'mere imminence or immediate futurity ... especially noticeable when it is co-ordinated with the future of another verb' (*Horn* II, 87) at ll. 291, 326. This last construction is considered characteristic of Anglo-Norman and is rare in O.F.

8. Introductory *que* is frequently absent before wish-clauses and commands in the third person, e.g. *Sovienge vus* 3, and also ll. 191, 297, 313, 314, 380, 402, 439, and occasionally in the first person sg., e.g. ll. 531, 892 (in ll. 69–72 the verbs probably depend on *prium* 65).

As is normal in O.F., the subjunctive is used in *St. Laurent* in subordinate clauses: (a) expressing will or purpose, whether substantival, as in ll. 60, 67, 69–72, 129, 254, 307, 324, etc.; adjectival, as in l. 833; consecutive with correlative *tel* or *si*, as in ll. 68, 315, 316, or without correlative, as in ll. 130, 189, 201, 944, 945; also in a deliberative indirect question in l. 759; (b) depending on a negative or otherwise non-affirmative principal, whether substantival, as in ll. 159, 433; adjectival, as in ll. 44, 342, 794, 813, 817, 943; consecutive, as in ll. 555, 587; (c) expressing concession, as in l. 52; (d) expressing anteriority in time, introduced by *ains que*, ll. 738, 912.

9. There is some use of parataxis, e.g. ll. 19–20, 201–2, 230, 420, 686–87, 864–65. Hypotaxis is more common, including consecutive clauses with correlatives such as *tant ... que* 395, 810–11, 815–16, etc. The locution *a poi, por poi* remains without analogical *que*, e.g. ll. 517, 615.

10. The style of *St. Laurent* includes the frequent use of Latin terms, presumably drawn from the Latin source text. The meaning of these Latin terms is often explained in the O.F. text, e.g. *laminas* ll. 631 ff., *catasta* 691 ff., *in agro Verano* 928–29, and *plunbatis* (found only in *B*) 666 ff. The author also draws on Latin liturgical and Biblical sources, e.g. *dispersit* 156, *Cui honor et gloria / Per seculorum*

secula 241–42, *Esse Jesum Filium Dei* 645. The use of proper names with Latin case-endings has been discussed above (Morphology, B).

V. Versification

1. Rhyme. *La Vie de St. Laurent* has 473 rhyming couplets. There seems to be a line, or lines, missing preceding l. 451, and between ll. 900 and 901. Feminine rhymes occur in 105 of the 473 couplets; 36 of the rhymes are rich, 17 are leonine. In one instance the poet has used the same rhyme in four consecutive lines, 351–54. The couplet is broken 25 times; enjambement is often used (e.g. ll. 93–94, 170–71, 297–98, 473–74, 561–62, 751–52, 919–20, etc.).
2. The Number of Syllables. By Central French standards, both manuscripts contain a number of faulty lines. Even after the use of dieresis or syneresis for contiguous vowels, of hiatus or elision of unstressed final *-e*, and discounting the scribal glide *e* in words such as *sov(e)rain(e)* 28, 317, 512 (but retaining it at l. 945), etc., there remain over 100 lines in the base manuscript which cannot be considered octosyllabic.[28] A further editorial emendation on the basis of variant readings from MS. *B*, and the substitution of longer or shorter doublet words *cumme/cum, ore/or*, etc., or the replacement of certain words with concurrent morphological forms, would permit the regularization of some of these lines.[29] There would still remain, however, 71 lines, or approximately 7½ per cent of the total, which are not octosyllabic by Central French rules.

These lines are as follows: ten syllables (2): 235, 677; nine syllables (18): 11, 138, 213, 263, 286, 321, 363, 369,

---

[28] Examples of the values allowed to arrive at this count are as follows: (a) dieresis: *nïent* 552, *passïon* 61, 77; (b) syneresis: one syllable counted for *nient* 47, 463, 465, 478; two syllables for *crestiens* 150, *eussent* 159, *passiun* 485, 486, *soliés* 225; four syllables for *Eclesiastes* 29; (c) elision: *ceo* 762, *jeo* 620, *ne < nec* 10, 283, *qui* 49, 277, 465, 720, 879, *se < si* 82, 163; (d) hiatus: *que iloc* 353, and the restoration in the syllable count of the *e* elided by the scribe in *quil* 254, 293, 296, 324, 398, 941.

[29] All these methods have been used by editors of Anglo-Norman texts in attempting to regularize the syllable count. See *Brendan*, pp. xiv ff., Schlyter, p. 29, Södergård, p. 60.

387, 388, 560, 644, 668, 742, 754, 857, 859, 910; seven
syllables, masculine (36): 24, 37, 126, 161, 167, 171, 195,
204, 219, 220, 256, 268, 284, 288, 292, 306, 434, 496,
501, 510, 520, 522, 526, 532, 535, 538, 578, 650, 665,
738, 748, 758, 846, 848, 875, 921; seven syllables, feminine
(12): 32, 36, 83, 127, 237, 281, 372, 447, 453, 467, 647,
794; six syllables (3): 115, 576, 687.

In arriving at the above figure of 71 'irreducible' lines, the
devices adopted in the interests of regularization (besides
the latitude in dieresis or syneresis mentioned above) are the
following. Variants from *B* have been admitted in ll. 50,
190, 277, 433, 436, 465, 495, 613, 671, 898, 919.[30] Sub-
stitution of doublet words has been assumed as follows: *ci*
for *ici* 20, 444, *contre* for *encontre* 200, *cum* for *cumme*
51 and 432 (both *cum* in *B*), 633, 836, 865, *cumme* for
cum 84 (*cumme* in *B*), 298 and 904 (both in hiatus), *encor*
for *encore* 745, *iceo* for *ceo* 55, *or* for *ore* 861, 867. Con-
current morphological forms assumed are: *beneeit* for
beneit 733, *el* for *ele* 60, *frai* for *ferai* 134, 179, 332, 561,
657, and *ier, iers* for *iere* 554, *ieres* 547. These lists do not
include lines which have been emended in the critical text
for reasons not purely metrical (211, 217, 258, 314, 440,
441, 443, 445, 946).

The 71 lines remaining after the possible emendations
listed above represent a relatively low proportion of the
total lines of the poem, and this suggests that the original
poem may have been written in 'correct' octosyllabics.
Many of the irregular lines lend themselves easily to correc-
tion; but the emendations would be sometimes drastic and

---

[30] MS. *B* is, however, more frequently metrically inferior to *A*, with 44 nine-
syllable lines, 40 seven-syllable masc. lines, 15 seven-syllable fem. lines, and 2 six-
syllable fem. lines not found in *A*, as follows: nine-syllable: 38, 48, 73, 75, 90, 98,
130, 173, 191, 198, 207, 234, 282, 304, 323, 356, 365, 399, 409, 416, 418, 422,
439, 454, 512, 527, 555, 584, 667, 685, 692, 731, 759, 763, 779, 782, 785, 795,
833, 842, 893, 900, 917, 918; seven-syllable masc.: 39, 106, 135, 172, 175, 203,
221, 223, 228, 280, 303, 312, 330, 352, 380, 402, 486, 487, 523, 549, 611, 631,
638, 654, 678, 693, 718, 749, 773, 788, 792, 831, 834, 839, 840, 869, 880, 902,
922, 936; seven-syllable fem.: 76, 80, 188, 246, 257, 308, 342, 349, 426, 457, 583,
646, 699, 798, 813; and six-syllable fem.: 451, 973. Some of the *B* variants are
metrically correct, but have inferior meanings (85, 230), or are morphologically
questionable (213).

always arbitrary.[31] As a result, none of the above regulari-
zation procedures has been used to emend metrically the
text of the poem.

3. Verse Structure. Scholarly opinion on the principles govern-
ing the caesura in octosyllabic verse in O.F. is divided.[32]
Not all the octosyllabic lines of *St. Laurent* can be divided
according to the sense into two parts of which the first ends
with a stressable tonic syllable; but in those which can be so
divided the commonest first hemistich is one of four syl-
lables (out of the first 100 octosyllables, some 36), then
those of three syllables (some 26) and of five syllables
(some 17). It is obvious that the verse structure is much less
rigid than that of the *Brendan*, in which 72 per cent of all
lines have the fourth syllable stressed;[33] nor does it con-
form closely to the caesural patterns proposed by A. T.
Baker for a number of Anglo-Norman texts, nor to that
found in *Le Petit Plet* by B. S. Merrilees.[34]

[31] In his edition, Söderhjelm admits ll. 235, 288 and 369 without emendation (*De Saint Laurent*, pp. v–xi), while regularizing the other lines (with the exception of ll. 36, 237, 387, which pass without comment although they remain irregular). Among the emendations he makes are the following, which affect our 71 'irreducible' lines (the manuscript reading is followed by / and the emendation): *ore/or* 11, *tuit/trestuit* 24, *nul ne/nul ne se* 32, *n'ait/n'en ait* 37, *alcuns/alcuns a* 55, *l'ara/l'en ara* 83, *car/car il* 115, *de/de mult* 126, *clers/clers fu* 127, *desque al/al* 138, *dona/il dona* 161, *bien/mult bien* 167, *dit/li dit* 171, *ai/ja ai* 195, *dunc/dunc l'a* 204, *destruite seies et/soies destruite e* 213, *mainent/enmainent* 219, *vient/i vient* 220, *ont/il ont* 256, *voloit/volt* 263, *out/out il* 268, *fu/il fu* 281, *mult/la mult* 284, *unt tant r./unt r.* 286, *que ne/que il ne* 292, *ydropici/e ydropici* 306, *les vertuz/vertuz* 321, *tote/trestote* 372, *amené/mené* 388, *mu/e mu* 434, *il/ton deu* 447, *que/que n'est* 453, *nostre/li nostre* 467, *fusmes/fusmes nos* 496, *la vie/vie e salu* 501, *mal/le mal* 510, *dunc/idunc* 520, *ont d./ont tot d.* 522, *par d./par grant d.* 526, *n'est/ne m'est* 532, *plus/mult plus* 535, *l'a/il l'a* 538, *ou il s./ou s.* 560, *fait/fait lever* 576, *fu/i fu* 578, *regehi/gehi* 644, *mund/munde* 647, *fait/fait dunc* 650, *l'unt/l'unt il* 665, *qui sunt/sunt* 668, *soit tot s./soit s.* 671, *v. del ciel qui/v. qui* 677, *c. maus ne t./c. les maus ne les t.* 687, *nul/nule* 738, *que iloc/qu'i* 742, *a c./a toz c.* 748, *une c./la c.* 754, *vunt/se vunt* 758, *huem/uns huem* 794, *dit/redit* 846, *sui/me sui* 848, *e. lei/l'e.* 857, *sunt/sunt or* 875, *sains/sains hom* 904, *s'en vunt/vunt* 910, *vint/en vint* 921.

[32] Cf. Georges Lote, *Histoire du vers français* (Paris, 1951), I, 233 ff.

[33] See *Brendan*, pp. xxxvii ff.

[34] See *Revue des langues romanes* LIX (1916–17), 256–59; and Chardri, *Le Petit Plet*, ed. B. S. Merrilees, A.N.T.S. XX (Oxford, 1970), p. xxviii.

DIALECT AND DATE

Apart from the many dialectal traits evident in spelling and versification, which may be purely scribal in the two extant copies of St. *Laurent*, the study of the forms in rhyme, above, has shown the following features, common in Anglo-Norman and Western O.F.: [ãn] and [ẽn] are separated in rhyme; the diphthong [ei] is retained. The reduction of [ie] to [e], and the replacement of masc. sg. nominative forms by masc. sg. accusative forms is characteristic principally of Anglo-Norman (but also of S.-W. O.F.). One syntactical trait, the periphrastic use of *voleir*, is frequent in the Anglo-Norman dialect. These above-mentioned traits, although few in number, indicate the Anglo-Norman origin of St. *Laurent*.

The following morphological and phonetic traits, found in both manuscripts, but not attested in rhyme, further suggest that St. *Laurent* belongs to the Anglo-Norman dialect: the masc. nom. sg. of unstressed possessives is *mis, tis, sis*; the termination of the first pers. pl. of the present tenses is without -*s* (-*um, -un, -on*); -*ge* is used in the singular of the pres. subj. (*muerges* 189, *sovienge* 3, *vienge* 315); the product of *paucum* is *poi*, not *pou*.

The attempt to assign the text a date of composition has to rely on linguistic evidence alone in the absence of any external evidence. As a result, any proposed date for the poem remains very tentative. A comparison of the linguistic characteristics of St. *Laurent* with those of other Anglo-Norman texts suggests a date in the later twelfth century, for the following reasons.

The development of rhymes between [ai] and [ei] offers the clearest indication of the relative chronological position of St. *Laurent*. In the last decade of the twelfth century [ai] and [ei] final are found in rhyme, as well as before [s], [st], [str], [r], [rə] in the works of Simund de Freine.[35] In the *Vie de St. Gilles*, dated approximately 1170, [ai] and [ei] are kept distinct in all positions, although [ai] rhymes with [ε] before [s] (as it does in St. *Laurent*), and [r].[36] Similarly, the *Vie d'Édouard le Confesseur* (1163–69) keeps [ai] and [ei] dis-

[35] Matzke, pp. xxiii ff.
[36] Ed. G. Paris, A. Bos, Paris, 1881, pp. xxvii ff.

tinct,[37] while in Beneit's *Vie de Thomas Becket* (1184) [ai] and [ei] rhyme before a consonant but not in final position.[38]

The lack of [ai] and [ei] rhymes before other than nasal consonants in *St. Laurent* suggests a date closer to the dates of the *Vies* of Giles and Edward the Confessor (i.e. *c.* 1170) than to the date of Beneit's *Thomas Becket*, or the works of de Freine. A tentative *terminus ad quem* then would be *c.* 1170. A possible *terminus a quo* is provided by Gaimar's *Estoire des Engleis*, dated in the period 1135—40.[39] Here [ai] rhymes with [ɛ] before [s] as it does in *St. Laurent*, and both texts have [ier] rhyming with [er], although the rhyme is quite rare in Gaimar. Rhymes in [ie] and [e] or [ier] and [er] are frequent in Thomas' *Romance of Horn* (dated *c.* 1170) and Beneit's *Thomas Becket*, but still infrequent in *St. Laurent, St. Gilles* and *Édouard*.[40]

The linguistic evidence, then, suggests a date in the third quarter of the twelfth century. Although the morphology affords an even less exact idea of date than the rhymes, the morphology of *St. Laurent* supports this approximate dating of the text. The breakdown in the declension system, most notable in the masc. sg. of parisyllabic nouns and adjectives, is similar to that found in *Édouard le Confesseur* and the *Romance of Horn*. Similarly, in the effacement of unstressed *e* in the future of *faire*, the usage in *St. Laurent* is also similar to that of *Horn* and *Édouard* (both *ferai* and *frai*, etc.).

The introduction of the glide *e* in the future of *aveir* is not found in *St. Laurent* and *Horn* but is found in *Édouard* and Beneit. Gaimar uses the *fer-* radical always, and has no glide *e*.

The syntax of *St. Laurent* offers no clear evidence of the date of the text. Apart from the periphrastic use of *voleir*, and the frequent use of the juxtaposed accusative to express possession (particularly popular in Anglo-Norman, cf. *Horn* II, 78), the syntax of *St. Laurent* shows no strong Anglo-Norman influence.

In summary, then, the linguistic evidence suggests a tentative date for *St. Laurent* somewhere in the period 1140—1170.

[37] Södergård, pp. 66 ff.
[38] Schlyter, pp. 42 ff.
[39] Ed. A. Bell, A.N.T.S. XIV—XVI, Oxford, 1960, pp. xxiv ff.
[40] *Horn* II, 37; Schlyter, pp. 42 ff.; *St. Gilles*, pp. xxviii ff.; Södergård, pp. 66 ff.

SOURCES

The legend of the martyrdom of St. Lawrence in Rome on
August 10, A.D. 258 was popular throughout the Middle Ages,
judging from the number of references made to this event by
medieval writers (as early as St. Ambrose), and from the num-
ber of versions of the legend, most extant in numerous manu-
script copies.[41]

The *Vie de St. Laurent* is the earliest known Old French
rhymed version of the legend.[42] The Latin source used by the
author of *St. Laurent* is the *Passio Polychronii* version, which
probably dates from the end of the fifth century.[43] For the
major part of the *Vie de St. Laurent* the author has clearly
followed the *P.P.* version (ll. 243—949 of *St. Laurent* corres-
pond to sections 19—29 of the *P.P.*, except for occasional com-
ments and interpolations by the author, discussed below). The
section of *St. Laurent* dealing with Sixtus occasionally intro-
duces details from abridged versions of the *P.P.* account not
found in the extended version. For example, the fact that
Sixtus has heard of the impending arrival in Rome of Decius (ll.
93—95, in the Latin *audiens Decium Romam esse venturum*);
the fact that Lawrence is summoned by Sixtus and entrusted
with the treasure of the Church immediately after Sixtus has
first announced the arrival of Decius to his clergy (ll. 125—31,
in the Latin *cum haec et his similia sancto suo sermone dis-*

---

[41] See the Bollandists' *Bibliotheca Hagiographica Latina Antiquae et Mediae
Aetatis* (Brussels, 1900—01), II, 708—12, and *Supplement* (Brussels, 1911), p. 187,
for a listing of the various versions, and the published editions. For the historical
basis of the legend and an account of early references to it see H. Delehaye, 'Recher-
ches sur le légendier romain', *Analecta Bollandiana* LI (1933), 34—72.

[42] A thirteenth-century French prose version is also extant. See Paul Meyer,
'Légendes hagiographiques en français. II. Légendes en prose', *Histoire littéraire de la
France* XXXIII (Paris, 1906), and by the same author, *Notices et extraits des manu-
scrits de la Bibliothèque nationale et autres bibliothèques* XXXV (1896), 484, 499;
XXXVI (1899), 44. Söderhjelm gives a brief account of later French dramatic ver-
sions, as well as of the preceding development of the legend; see *De saint Laurent*, pp.
xvii—xxxv.

[43] See *Analecta Bollandiana* LI (1933), 70—71. This version is found in a great
many manuscript copies; an accessible text has been published by Delehaye at the
end of his article describing the historical development of the legend, mentioned
above, op. cit., pp. 72—98. All further references to the *Passio Polychronii* version
(abbreviated *P.P.*) will be to this published text.

seruisset, vocavit sanctum Laurentium archidiaconum suum, civem Romanum, dignum Deo virum, et habitu, et vultu, et sanctitate conspicuum, et tradidit ei omnes facultates Ecclesiae dicens: Sint haec penes te diligenti cura reposita, quatenus non possit ad ea avari regis cupiditas pervenire); and the fact that Lawrence sold the treasures of the Church (l. 150, in the Latin *tunc beatus Laurentius omnia quae perceperat christianis artificibus vendidit et omne pretium pauperibus erogavit*).[44]

At other points in the narrative, the *Vie de St. Laurent* presents details from the full *P.P.* account in a new sequence; for example, the exchange between Lawrence and Sixtus, ll. 132–40 (*P.P.* section 13), precedes the account of the distribution of the treasure to the poor and the exchange between Sixtus and Decius, ll. 169–207 (*P.P.* section 12).

Similarly, the question of Lawrence, ll. 224–26 (*P.P.* section 13: *Quo progrederis sine filio, pater? . . . Tu numquam sacrificasti sine ministro nec offerre consueveras*) is not introduced until the moment he is about to be arrested, ll. 228–29 (*P.P.* section 18).

In the part of the narrative dealing with Sixtus, then, the author of *La Vie de St. Laurent* has arranged and condensed his source material; this part of the legend serves as a long introduction which sets the scene for the description of the martyrdom of Lawrence. In that part of his narrative, as mentioned above, the author has followed his Latin source quite closely, with some expansion and commentary.

The additions to and commentaries made on the Latin sources by the Anglo-Norman author are mainly didactic. These include the prologue (ll. 1–92) which begins with a section remarkably similar to the *Exhortatio Auctoris* (ll. 161–180) of the *Cumpoz* of Philippe de Thaon. (In both poems the author invokes the attention of and correction by his *maistre*, illustrating this plea by a theme from Ecclesiasticus on true friendship

---

[44] These details are found in the versions classified as 2b, c, d in the *Bibliotheca Hagiographica Latina* II, 1130. These versions are found in many manuscripts including Paris, Bibliothèque nationale, Latin 5306, fos. 212ʳ–213ʳ, Latin 17002, fos. 40ʳ–41ᵛ; London, British Library, Latin 11880, fos. 21ª–24ª, etc. A transcription of the latter has been published by P. A. Lagarde, *Hippolyti Romani Quae Feruntur Omnia Graece* (Leipzig and London, 1858), pp. xiii–xvi. See also *Analecta Bollandiana* XI (1892), 289–90.

becoming evident in time of need.) The author of *St. Laurent* next introduces and develops the contrast between the vanity of earthly things and the eternity of pain (Hell) and glory (Heaven), ll. 19—37, this time borrowing from the Bible (Ecclesiastes). This is followed by a lament for the vanished qualities and achievements of former heroes which links classical and Biblical characters as a further illustration of the vanity of earthly endeavours and possessions (ll. 38—58). The work about to be created by the author is invoked as a means of salvation, as a permanent good work (ll. 59—74). It is stated that the poem has been undertaken *por une ancele saint Lorenz* (l. 76), as an aid to her salvation, as indeed the story of St. Lawrence can save anyone who pays close heed to it and mends his ways. The historical background is sketched (ll. 85—92), then the narrative begins (l. 93).

From time to time the author strengthens the moral lesson of the legend by reference to Biblical quotations, which are sometimes commented upon, as at ll. 153—68, 344, 349—53, 851—53, 870—73. The author's comments on the sharing of the wealth of the Church with the poor (ll. 153—68) include explanations of motives and thoughts (e.g. *Il set bien que li tirant / S'i prendrunt mal vers lui par tant* 167—68).

Similarly, elsewhere in the text, statements of motives are made which are absent or merely implied in the Latin versions. It is stated, for example, that Lawrence does not reply to Decius during the first interrogation, *Car il voloit le felon tirant / Conmoveir en ire par tant* 263—64, as opposed to the Latin: *Beatus Laurentius non respondidit ei verbum* (*P.P.*, section 19). The author also gives a reason (however vague) for the imprisonment of Lucillus: *Ki fait out ne sei quel otrage / Et por ceo fu enprisoné* 278—79, and for the duration of the imprisonment, ll. 280—84; the Latin has simply *Erat autem ibi homo in custodia multo tempore, gentilis, qui plorando amissis oculis caecus factus fuerat* (*P.P.*, section 20). The author's wish to explain events seems to have inspired the long commentary on the conversion of Hippolytus (ll. 333—59). The miracle is explained in terms of the religious beliefs of the time, supported by two Biblical quotations.

The longest section that can be attributed to the invention of

the Anglo-Norman writer is the expansion of the distinction to be made between *faiture* and *creature*, ll. 444—515. The idea that God is the supreme creator is made more explicit by reference to the Biblical account of the creation of the universe (ll. 456—71). The statement of the fallen nature of Man (ll. 472—74) is followed by a discourse on the Divine plan for the redemption of Man, including the Virgin Birth, the Passion, and a short development of the theme of the contrast between the death-giving tree of knowledge and the life-giving tree of the Cross. (This latter is also a medieval commonplace.)[45] Once again the author has attempted to explain, in the religious terms of the audience, the point raised by the complicated debate on *creature* and *faiture*, using a short synopsis of relevant Christian dogma to do so.

This last major didactic interpolation in the narrative has been presented through the character of Saint Lawrence, and as such, it marks a sophistication in didactic technique; by including it as part of the debate between Lawrence and his tormentors, the poet makes the didactic comment an integral part of the legend. The struggle between the saint and the emperor is placed in the wider context of the whole of Christian dogma and the greater conflict between good and evil. The debate form used by the author of *St. Laurent* to portray this conflict is a traditional one in Anglo-Norman hagiography.[46] With the exception of the development of the *faiture—creature* theme, however, which is allowed to slow down the dramatic movement of the piece, the debates in *St. Laurent* are not highly developed or lengthy disputations, but rather are quickly paced, and the account of the martyrdoms is related with economy and some dramatic intensity, culminating in the final torture on the grill and the famous reply of Lawrence: *Chaitif, l'altre part car tornez; / Mangez deça, quit est assez* 896—97.

---

[45] See M. Dominica Legge, *Anglo-Norman Literature and its Background* (Oxford, 1963), p. 252.

[46] Cf. for example *The Life of St. Catherine by Clemence of Barking*, ed. W. MacBain, A.N.T.S. XVIII, Oxford, 1964, and 'St. Georges' in *Les Œuvres de Simund de Freine*, ed. J. E. Matzke, Paris, 1909.

ESTABLISHMENT OF THE TEXT

The scribe of the base MS. *A* uses few abbreviations, all of which are common and readily verified from forms of the words written in full, with the exception of 7 which has been transcribed as *et*. The scribe of MS. *B*, however, uses numerous superscripts, many of which stand for two or more abbreviated forms. For example, the superscript 7 has been resolved as both *re* (*prent* 47, *prendre* 79, etc.) and *er* (*adversitez* 10, *merci* 56, etc.); superscript *a* has been resolved as *ra* (*grant* 35, etc.) and *ua* (*quant* 7, etc.), as well as *ru* (*destrueit* 91, *cruelté* 99) on the basis of *crute* 754 (written in full at l. 926); superscript *e* has been resolved as *re* (*demustrez* 15, *prendre* 101, etc.) or *ue* (*quer* 49, *purquei* 564, etc.); superscript *i* is transcribed *ri* (*escrit* 3, *crime* 88, etc.) or *ui* (*qui* 47, 49, *quil* 52, etc.); the superscript 2 is resolved as *es* in *Jhesu*, or *eu* (*Deus* 38, etc.), or *ue* (*que* 4, 155, etc.), or *ar* (*kar* 103, 781); the abbreviated form of *Jhesu* ends in *u* or *c* (ll. 111, 507, 513, 646).

The critical text has been normalized according to the standard modern conventions, including the use of capitals, punctuation, and the regularization of *i* and *j*, *u* and *v*, *c* and *ç*. The acute accent is used on the letter *e* in the endings *e* and *es* when the *e* is not atonic, and to distinguish *Dé* from *de*. The diaeresis has not been used, however, because of the uncertainty of the intended metre. Latin words and phrases used in the poem are printed in italics, except for proper names declined in isolation, discussed in Morphology, *B*, above. Divisions in the text, made in the same places in both manuscripts by ornamented initial capital letters, are shown by indentation in the text (ll. 75, 93, 169, 243, 319, 381, 411, 536, 614, 756, 770, 786, 854, 868, 908). Corrections to the manuscript text consisting of an additional letter, letters or words appear in square brackets and are not otherwise indicated. Rejected readings of the base manuscript appear at the foot of the page; those variant readings of MS. *B* which affect the sense, metre or morphology of the text are printed together before the Notes; where the reading of *B* has been adopted in the text, it is not listed in the Variants. Purely orthographical variants are excluded, including the following consistent differences: MS. *B* has *aver* for *A*'s *aveir*, and

similarly *ben* for *bien*, *ert* for *iert*, *fet* for *fait*, *nent* for *nient*, *pot* for *puet*, *ren* for *rien*, *sens* for *sanz*, *sur* for *sus*, *valt* for *vaut*, *vet* for *vait*, *vols* for *veus*, and *volt* for *veut*.

LA VIE DE SAINT LAURENT

LA VIE DE SAINT LAURENT

Maistre, a cest besoing vus dreciez
Et mei cumme deciple aidiez.
Sovienge vus d'icel escrit
4   Ke Jesus le fiz Sirac dit:
Ja en nule prosperité
N'iert amis verai esprové;
Mais quant il a de lui mester
8   Dunc puet son ami esprover,
Car en besoing n'iert ja celez;
Ne anemis en aversitez,
Car quant le veit en l'ore del mal
12   Idunc l'enpeint de munt el val.
Amis al besoing se descuevre,
Et enemis al mal se coivre.
A cest besoing vus demostrez,
16   Ou mesdit ai, si m'amendez.
Plus sage de mei puet mesdire
En mains k'a traiter tel martire.
Bien me aperceif quant me porpens
20   Ici ne seron que un poi de tens.
Ne sei dont li mund nos encumbre;
Ceste vie n'est fors un umbre
Que nos deceit et trait a mort;
24   Tuit muerent, et fier et fort.
Vie est brieve, li mund muablez,
Gloire et peine sunt parmanablez.
Chascuns dei[t] eschever la peine
28   Et traire a la gloire soveraine.
Eclesiastes fiz David dit,
La ou il vanité descrit,
Que tot perist, rien n'en renueve
32   Ne novelté nul ne trueve.
Nul ne puet la richeise aveir

Qu'autre n'ait eu tel aveir.
Ore n'a nul si grant richeise,
36   Saveir, bealté, ne proueise
Que altre n'ait plus eu.
E Deus! qu'est ore devenu
Le grant sen Aristotilis,
40   La richeise dan Cesaris,
Le pris et la force Sanson,
Et la grant bealté Apsalon?
Que vaut [desir]? Que vaut voleir?
44   Que vaut delit c'um puisse aveir?
Que vaut la joie de cest munt?
Trestoz deliz a nient revunt;
Tot vient de nient, a nient revert.
48   Ki trop i prent, son tens i pert.
Fous est qui en aveir sun cuer fiche,
Car tuit muerent, povre et riche,
Et li sages cumme li fols muert,
52   A un vienent que qu'il demuert;
Par une vaie tuit en vunt.
Riens ne vei durable en cest munt
Fors ceo ke alcuns bien fait
56   Dunt aprés sa mort merci ait,
Ou los ou pris d'alcune ovraigne
Qui en cest siecle lui parmaigne.
Et por ceo vos en cummenz une
60   Et pri qu'ele soit a toz cummune,
De la passion, des tormenz,
Ke por Deu sosfri saint Lorenz,
Cum il fu por s'amor penez
64   Et a martire demenez.
Or prium Deu que por s'amour, $1^v a$
Cum il por lui sosfri dolour,
Qu'il nos doinst faire tele ovraigne
68   Ke nos ames nen aient peine,
Mes sa grace entre nos descende
Et nos cors d'enconbrer defende

34 a. autel a.   35 nest nule

Des feluns engins al deable,
72 Et joie nos donst parmanable
El regné de sa maesté
Ou vit, et regne, en Trinité.

Ceste ovre faz que ci conmenz
76 Por une ancele saint Lorenz
Qui sa passion et s'estoire
Veut por lui aveir en memoire,
A ses faiz veut essample prendre.
80 Qui de bon cuer i veut entendre
De folor se puet bien retraire;
Et se il veut son servise faire,
Deu l'ara en sa grant gloire,
84 Si cum lisum en l'estoire
Del beneuré Syxte, un produmme.
Quant fu apostoile de Rumme,
Fu le plus del mund paenime
88 Et li homme erent plain de crime.
Deable par sa covoitise
Out envie de sainte iglise,
Ses membres partot destruieit
92 Par ceus qu'en poesté aveit.

Syxtus oi d'un felun home
Dire que dut venir a Rumme;
Decius Cesar out a non.
96 Alez ert par la region
Por destruire crestienté;
Or vait vers Rome la cité.
Par sa cruele cuvertise
100 Quide destruire sainte iglise;
Al chef se vout prendre premier,
Les altres voloit esmaïer.
Car qui la racine destruit
104 De la raimne vaut poi le fruit.
Destruire veut le fondement,

$1^v b$

77 se estoire

Et saint Syxte tres bien l'entent.
Il asemble tot son clergié
108   De Rumme al chief de l'evesché;
Cumforte les, si lor sarmone
Ke prest soient de la corone
Que Jesus a as suens pramis
112   En cel regné de parais,
Et dit: 'Fiz, soiés en Deu fort.
Ne dotez por lui sofrir mort,
Car por nos la susfri,
116   Resusfrum la por lui issi.
Decius Cesar vient sus nos,
Mei departira ja de vos.
Vos qui aprés mei remaindrez,
120   Amés Deu et sa lei tenez!'
Feliscissimus dit a lui
Et Agapitus, diacre andui:
'Bel pere, ou irez vos sens nos,
124   Et nos, que devendrum senz vos?'
Syxtus apele saint Lorenz
Qui fu nez de bones genz,
Bons clers, riches, et diacnes.
128   De Rumme esteit archidiacnes.
Dit lui que toz les tresors gart, $2^r a$
Que Decius n'i ait ja part:
'Tote la cure en met sus tei.'
132   Lorenz dit: 'Ou irez senz mei?
Senz vostre fiz ou en alez?
Pere, que ferai? car m'en menez!
Aprés vos que ferai jeo ci?'
136   Et saint Syxte lui respondi:
'Del mien aler n'aies tristour.
Ensemble seron desque al tiers jor;
Ne te guerpis, tu me sevras,
140   Tresque al ters jor o moi seras.'
Grant miracle fu d'icest dit
Qu'il en sa mort l'altrui mort vit.

117 viens   142 Qui en

De lui saveit que morir dut
144 Et la mort de saint Lorenz sut.
Saint Lorenz la fin de sa vie
A entendu par prophecie.
L'or de l'iglise et tot l'argent
148 En vessele et en vestement,
Quanque pout trover, tot fait prendre
Et a[s] crestiens le vait pois vendre.
Toz les povres a asemblé,
152 L'aveir lor a por Deu doné.
La grace de lui deservi,
Al vers del salter entendi
Que danz David prophetiza:
156 *Dispersit*, povres le dona.
Sa justise en maint parmanable,
Ne veut que li menbre al deable
Eussent l'aveir de sainte iglisse,
160 Ci fist resonable justise
Quant dona por l'amor Dé
L'aveir qui lui fu commandé;
Car se en sa garde trové fust
164 A l'oes Deu gardé pas ne l'eust.
Es membres Deu l'a despendu
Et cil l'unt mangé et beu.
Il set bien que li tirant
168 S'i prendrunt mal vers lui par tant.

La ou li clerc sunt asemblé
Decius o tot le sené
Vient et dit: 'Syxte, sez tu
172 Por quei nos summes ci venu?'
Syxte respont: 'Oil, tres bien!'
Decius dit: 'O nos dunc vien,
Sacrefise a [nos] deu[s] feras
176 Ou [si] ce non, ici morras.'
Syxtus respunt: 'Lur sacrefis?
Deu sacrefierai toz dis;

$2^r b$

164 p. ne fust   169 siunt   177 lui

A vos deus ne ferai sacrefice
180 Por poor ne por covoitise,
Car rien n'entendent, si sunt mu;
Quanque om lor fait, si est perdu.
Dunt ne sunt il d'or et d'argent?'
184 Quant Decius iceo entent,
De maltalant tressue et de ire.
Nequedent si lui prent a dire:
'Pren conseil, change ton corage;
188 Aies merci de ton aage,
Que ne muerges par ta folor,
Ne ne metes les tuens en error.
Male essample n'aient de tei.
192 Crei ceo ke deguerpis ta lei,
Mult grant richeise te dorai
Et sus les tuens te eshaucerai.'
Sixtus dit: 'Conseil ai pris;
196 Tes deus refus, tes leis guerpis.
Jeo crei en Deu de bon corage;
Tant cumme sui de graindre aage
De tant doi jeo miex Deu servir
200 Et sa lei encontre toz tenir,
Ke nul ne puisse dire aprés
Ma lei en ma veillesse les.'
Quant Decius iceo entent
204 Dunc conmande a sa gent
Tresque al temple Martis mener.
S'il ne veut son deu aorer,
Le chief lui commande a trenchier.
208 Dunt l'en mainent li chevalier
Al temple Martis a s'image.
Saint Sixte dit o fier corage:
'Ymage qui n'os ne [ne] veiz,
212 Tu qui la fole gent deceiz,
Destruite soies et confondue!'
Une grant part est donc chaue
De l'orible temple Martis,
216 Et li chevaler Cesaris

$2^v a$

Sunt cummeu par tant a ire
Et mainent saint Sixte a martire.
La ou il mainent le saint
220　Saint Lorenz vient, si l'ataint.
Dit lui: 'Bel pere, que ferai?
Toz les tresors despenduz ai.
As povres Deu les ai donez.
224　Pere, senz mei ou en alez?
Quant soliés faire sacrefise　　　　　　　　$2^v b$
Que ne fusse a vostre servise?'
Quant li serjant ont ceo oi,
228　De totes pars l'en ont saisi
Por les tresors qu'il reconut
Quant dist as povres donez les ut.
Funt lei garder a un serjant
232　Et mainent dunt saint Sixte avant
A une part desos le mont
Et deus compaignons que o lui sunt,
Felicisscimus et Agapitus,
236　Dunt jeo fiz mencion lasus.
Toz treis iloc decolerent.
Crestiens les cors enterrerent.
Funderent i puis un moster
240　Por Deu servir et deprier
Cui honor et gloria
Per seculorum secula.

Puis la mort Sixte l'apostoile
244　Li chevaler del Capitoile
Tindrent saint Lorenz le diacre,
Le tresorer archidiacne.
A Decium est dunc venu
248　Artimius qui tribuns fu
Et dit: 'Sire, vostre serjant
Ont retenu un mescreant
Qui lors tresors a a garder.
252　Jeo l'ai oi Lorenz nonmer.'

217 cummuz　　　220 latant

Decius dit: 'Va al prevost
Et di lui qu'il l'amaint tost.'
Cil s'en torne et dit lui tant;
256 Quant ont oi le conmant,
Les mains liees le menerent   3ra
Et Decio le presenterent.
Decius mult se esleeça
260 Por le[s] tresor[s] qu'il coveita;
Demande et enquiert ou il sunt,
Et saint Lorenz riens ne respunt,
Car il voloit le felon tirant
264 Conmoveir en ire par tant.
Decius ot qu'il ne dit rien.
Livrer le fait a Valerien
Qui ert prevost de la cité,
268 Sus toz out grant poosté.
Dit lui que bonement essait
K'il lui die que fait en ait.
Valerien le livre avant
272 A Ypolite, un suen serjant
Qui desos lui vicaire estait.
La jaiole en sa garde aveit.
Mena lei dreit a sa maison.
276 Saint Lorenz trueve en la prison
Un paen qui ert de grant parage,
Ki fait out ne sei quel otrage,
Et por ceo fu enprisoné.
280 Grant piece i avoit ja esté;
Por ceo que fu debonaire
Nel voloit justise desfaire,
Ne il ne l'ossent lesser aler
284 Mais le funt mult dur garder.
De la dolor qu'il a eu
Et de ceo qu'il l'unt tant retenu
A tant ploré que riens ne veit.
288 Lucillus sis nuns esteit.
Mult lungement a esté cius.   3rb

258 et a d.   271 le leure a.   273 uuicaire

Dunt lui dist saint Lorenz, li pius,
Que se en Jesu croire veut
292 Il vera miex que ne seut.
Lucillus dit qu'il veut croire;
Saint Lorenz le baptise en aire,
Et Deu lui rendi la veue
296 Qu'il devant ceo out perdue.
Lucillus dit: 'Loés en soit
Jesu Crist, cum estre deit,
Qu'il me deigna revisiter,
300 Par saint Lorenz enluminer.
Anceis fui ciu et ore vei,
Jesu Crist, graces rent a tei!'
La renommee par tot vait
304 Et vienent ciu, vienent contrait,
Fievreus et *paralitici*,
Languissans *ydropici*.
Prient lui que merci lor face;
308 Et Jesu Crist par sa grant grace
Rent santé a toz por s'amor.
Rendun l'en graces et honor
Des vertus, des signes, des biens
312 Qu'il a fait por toz crestiens.
Loé soit Deu et sa puissance;
A nos doinst faire tel faisance,
Que lui vienge si a plaisir
316 Que a sa gloire puissum venir
Et aveir la joie soveraine
Ou l'en avra delit senz paine.

Ypolitus qui les prisuns
320 Out a garder en ses maisuns,
Ot les miracles et les vertuz
Qui sunt iloques avenuz.
Vient a la chartre et dit al saint
324 Qu'il les tresors lui ensaint.
Et saint Lorenz idunc lui dist,

3^{v}a

314 tele

Se croire veut en Jesu Crist,
Que les tresors lui mostrera
328   Et vie parmanable avra.
Quant Ypolite iceo oi
A saint Lorenz tost respondi:
'Se tes dis fas et aconplis
332   Jeo ferai ceo que tu m'as requis.'
Ohi, Jesus, reis tot puissanz,
Tant par sunt tes miracles granz!
Petit covient a sarmoner
336   Home que tu veus espirer;
Se vers tei s'atorne de rien,
Tost l'as mué del mal al bien.
Qui a tei torne son corage,
340   Poi doit doter perte ou damage,
Ou peril ou paine ou angoisse,
Ou mal que nul faire lui poisse.
L'evangile dit a estros:
344   Se Deu por nos, qui contre nos?
O qui Deus est, poi puet chaleir
D'altrui orguel, d'altrui saveir.
Car nos trovon aillors escrit,
348   Ou Deus a ses apostres dit:
'Quant vos vendrés as reis, as contes,
Devant prevos, devant viscontes,
Que devez dire, ne pensez,
352   Car a l'ore vos iert donez
Iceo que iloc parlerez.' 3vb
De Ypolite oi avez,
Qui soloit tormenter les genz,
356   Cum respunt bel a saint Lorenz.
Deus out son cuer mult tost mué
Et son corage a lui torné
Et de sa grace repleni.
360   Saint Lorenz son respons oi.
Les funs fait dunc apareiller
Et beneistre et seigner.
Lorenz dist: 'Crois tu en Jesu Crist?'
364   '*Credo*,' Ypolitus lui dist.

'Et qu'il est Deus Peres et Fiz
Et que il soit saint Esperiz?'
'*Credo*,' Ypolitus respunt.
368   A itant treis fais plumgé l'unt
En figure de la Trinité;
En Deu l'unt si regeneré.
Saint Lorenz a pois sa mesnee
372   O lui tote baptisee.
Tot par nonbre dis et nuef furent
Qui por Deu baptesme reçurent,
Par la doutrine saint Lorenz.
376   Por Deu ourent puis granz tormenz
Cum orez avant en l'estoire.
Deu en soit l'onor et la gloire;
De toz les biens que a fait por nos
380   Loez en soit sis nuns precious!

Decius a dunc cummandé
Que saint Lorenz soit amené.
Valerien mander le fait.
384   Ypolite a la chartre vait
Et dit lui: 'Lorenz, beals amis,
Valerien m'a ça tramis.
De part Decii m'est conmandé
388   Que devant lui soies amené.'
Saint Lorenz respont: 'Ambedui
En alum ore desque a lui.
Ne dotun lui, ne sa mesnee,
392   Car grant gloire est apareillee
A mei et a vos ensement.'
Andui en vunt dunc liement.
Tant ont alé qu'il sunt venu
396   Al siege ou Valerien fu.
Valerien dit dunc al saint
Qu'il les tresors lui ensaint.
Saint Lorenz dit: 'Or me donez
400   Treis jors de terme, ses verrez.'
Valerien dist: 'Otrié
Te soit si cumme l'as prié.'

$4^r a$

Decio dit qu'il en a fait.
404 Et saint Lorenz d'iloc s'en vait.
Par la cité fait asembler
Toz les povres qu'il puet trover,
Ou les tresors out despendu —
408 Il l'unt ja mangé et beu —
Et muce les en la maisun
Ypolite, son compaignun.

Decius Cesar al tiers jor
412 Se sist al sié l'enpereor.
Li barun del sené i sunt;
Tienent plait et jugement funt,
Quant Lorenz i a amené
416 La povre gent que out asemblé,
Et dit oiant trestoz en haut: 4^{r}b
'Ves ci le tresor qui ne faut,
Descreistre ne puet, ains creistra,
420 Tiex est ja n'amenuisera.'
Et Valerien en est desvez;
Veant Decio est levez,
Oiant toz dit a saint Lorenz:
424 'Guerpis, va! tes enchantemenz,
Et fai a nos deus sacrefise,
Ou nos ferun de tei justise!
A nos deus sacrefieras
428 Ou a torment ocis seras!'
Saint Lorenz dit al mescreable:
'Ohi, tu, membre de deable,
A quei dis tu que crestien
432 Aort deable cumme paen?
Nen est lei que crestien aort
Tel deu qui est mu et sort,
Car d'or sunt, d'argent et d'araim,
436 Et si sunt sort, mu, et vain.
Sainte Escripture idles les nunme
Car faiture sunt de main d'unme;

403 diceo   418 li t.

Or soit sus vous le jugement;
440 Quel doit aorer tote gent,
Ou ceo qu'om fait ou cil quis fait?
Decius dit: 'Ceo conment vait?
Ki est qui fait, et k'om fait qui?'
444 Lorenz dit: 'Ton deu que vei ici
Est ceo qu'om fait, et ne fait rien,
Car il ne fait ne mal ne bien.
Il est fait cumme faiture;
448 Ceo que fait est, la creature
Ne doit par raison aorer,   4ᵛa
Ne son Creator aviler.
Car quant ceo que l'en fait aore,
452 Sei avile, car creature
Est plus haute que faiture.
Ouevre d'alcun est ceo qu'en fait,
Mais Deu fait tot, par lui tot vait.
456 Il est qui fait, car tote ovraigne
Fist es sis jors de la semaine,
Cum el salter trovun escrit
Que tot fu fait des qu'il out dit;
460 Tresque son plesir out mandé
Si fu quanque est, ou fu, crié.
Qui tot cria par ceo qu'il dist,
Est qui fait, car tot de nient fist.'
464 Decius Cesar lui respont:
'Qui est qui de nient fist tot le mund?'
Saint Lorenz dit: 'Deu, Nostre Pere,
Jesu Crist, Nostre Salvere,
468 Crieres est de tot le munde;
Ciel et mer et terre rounde,
Enfers et li quatre element,
Vunt tot par son commandement.
472 E geter nos veut de la paine
Ou tuit estoient par l'estreine
De Adam et de Evam sa moillier.
Por nos tolir de l'Averser

440 aveir   441 que homme   443 ke homme; Qui *begins l. 444*
445 que homme   473 estriene

476 Cuntre nature par puissance
    Prist de la Virge dunc naissance.
    Par poesté, nient par nature,
    Se fist Creator creature.
480 Deus engendra son Fiz senz Mere,
    Virge conçut son Fil senz Pere,
    Virge conçut, Virge out enfant. $4^v b$
    Virge fu pois, Virge devant.
484 Por la nostre redempciun
    Sosfri Nostre Sire passiun.
    De sa passiun et de sa mort
    Nos fu et vie et confort,
488 Car sa mort et sa passiun
    Nos fu de mort redempciun.
    Icele mort, mort ne fu mie,
    Ains fu salu de mort a vie;
492 Car par la passiun Jesu
    Avun nos confort et salu.
    Mort nos dona li premiers fruiz,
    Vie nos dona icist en cruiz;
496 Par fust fusmes tuit perdu,
    Par fust ravun vie et salu.
    Cum cel arbre porta le fruit
    Par unt nos fusmes tuit destruit,
500 Icest arbre le fruit porta
    Qui la vie nos dona.
    Cel porta la mort en la pome
    Et cest, vie en la char de homme.
504 Cil morut qui cel fruit manja;
    Qui cest manjue, si vivra
    En la gloire de parais
    Ou te, Jesus, regnes et vis.
508 Al grant Juise revendras
    Et bons et maus dunc jugeras.
    Qui mal unt fait, mal avrunt;
    Le bien avrunt qui bien fait unt,
512 Lasus en cel soverain regné

481 conut

Ou Jesus vit en Trinité
Ki serf jeo sui, qui jeo aour   5ra
Et qui jeo tieng por Creator.'
516   Quant Decius Cesar l'entent
A poi ne muert de maltalant.
Dunc le conmande a despoiller
Et faire batre d'aiglenter.
520   Dunc vunt faire li serjant
Le conmandement al tirant.
Saint Lorenz ont desvestu;
Batent lei d'aiglenter tot nu.
524   Trestot le cors lui funt sanglent.
La ou il est en cel torment
Si dit en haut par douçour:
'Graces rent a Deu mon Seignour
528   Qui m'a issi revisité
Et de sa grace enluminé
Que o ses sers me veut ajoster.
Jesu, tei puisse jeo loer,
532   Cïst batre n'est torment pas.'
A Decium dit: 'Ohi, las!
Chaitis, en ire forsenés,
Et plus de mei tormentés!'

536   Decius veit qu'il el ne fera.
En halt lever le conmanda.
Quant l'a fait en halt lever,
Devant lui fait puis aporter
540   Fors tormenz de totes manieres,
De fust, de fer, de plun, de pieres.
Onques ne fu nul torment fait
Que al feel Deu mostré nen ait.
544   Decius dit a saint Lorenz:
'Et ne veis tu toz ces tormenz
Ke por tei sunt ci aporté?   5rb
Tu ieres en chascun tormenté
548   Se ne veus nos deus aorer
Et ta fole eror delaisser.'
Saint Lorenz al tormenteor:

'Ton deu refus, le mien aour!
552 Ces paines ne criem jeo nient.
A mei sunt gloire, a tei torment.
Ja n'iere por Deu en tel destrait,
Douce viande ne me soit.'
556 Et Decius dunc lui demande:
'Quant torment t'est douce viande,
Ou sunt dunc li escumengé,
Li fol crestien renoié?
560 Di ou il sunt, enseigne les moi!
Ferei les venir manger o tei
La viande que loes tant.'
Saint Lorenz respunt al tirant:
564 'Aprés ices por quei demandes?
Il n'unt talant de tes viandes,
Ne n'ont de tes tormenz peour;
Lors nuns sunt ja o lor Seignor
568 Escris en paradis lasus.'
Decius le fait metre jus.
Lié le fait mener o lui
Tresque al paleis Tyberii,
572 Por oir en commune oance
Iceo qu'a fait en sa creance.
Et Decius al temple vait,
Son tribunal lever i fait.
576 Quant il out fait son sié,
Por saint Lorenz a envoié;
Tout le sené o lui fu.   5^{v}a
Quant saint Lorenz i est venu,
580 Decius dit: 'Lai ta folie.
Envers nos deus te humelie.
Fai lor honor et sacrefise
Ou de ton cors ferai justise.
584 N'afier tant en tes tresors
Ke l'en a hunte maint ton cors;
Car ja n'iert ton tresor si grant
K'il contre mort te soit garant.

569 maitre

588   Escheve des tormenz la peine
        Et les tresors avant ameine,
        Et di ou li crestien sunt
        Qui nostre deu en vilté unt.
592   Ocire les voil et pener
        Et la cité de els delivrer.
        Guerpis t'esrour et si la lei
        Et sacrefi[s]e a nos deus fei!
596   N[e] quider pas que ton aveir
        Te puisse encontre mei valeir,
        Ne richoise d'or ne d'argent
        Te defende de mon torment.
600   En ton tresor granment t'afies
        Quant a nos deus ne sacrefies.'
        Et saint Lorenz lui respundi:
        'Veirs est, en mon tresor m'afi
604   Que nule peour n'ai de tei.
        En cil m'afi en qui jeo crei.
        En mon tresor ai esperance
        Que tei ne dot ne ta faisance.
608   Crei al tresor celestien
        Que ne dout torment terrien.
        Ne l'avras ja par nul torment; $5^{v}b$
        Doné l'ai tot a povre gent.
612   Deu m'iert garant; bon confort ai.
        Quanque faire me pues, ore me fai.'

         Quant l'entent Decius Cesar,
        Por poi ne muert d'ire et d'eschar.
616   Dunc le fait batre et tormenter
        Et de grans fuz grans cous doner.
        Saint Lorenz dit ens el torment:
        'Jesus, Sire, graces t'en rent
620   De ceste joie que jeo ore ai
        Et de cele que apruef arai!
        Cruel tirant, or pues veer
        Qu'en mon tresor ai bon espeir;

609 tei *expuncted after* que

624 Sus tes tormenz ai ja vitoire,
La paine que jeo sent m'est gloire.
Quanque tu fais, si m'est delit!'
Decius dunc s'escrie et dit:

628 'Tu es tot plain d'enchantemenz;
Par ceo sormontes nos tormenz.
Un altre torment ore avras.'
Dunc fait aporter *laminas*:

632 Ceo est mult orible torment,
Si cumme dient romaine gent;
Ceo sunt platines de fer granz.
Dunc les fait metre li tiranz

636 Ardantes al costé del saint.
Tot art et brusle quanque ataint.
Art lui les costés et le dos,
La char lui brusle tresque as os.

640 Dunc dit: 'Jesus Deus, verai rei,
Aiez, Sire, merci de mei!
Quant por ton nun acusé fui   6ra
Ne te neai, ains te conui;

644 Quant demanderent, tei regehi
Esse Jesum Filium Dei.
Tu es Jesus Deus, verai Peres,
Et de tot le mund Salveres.'

648 Decius veit que ses tormenz
Ne valent rien; mult est dolenz.
Les plateines fait oster
Et lui de la terre lever,

652 Et dit au barun saint Lorenz:
'En tei vei art d'enchantemenz.
Se tu mes tormenz destruit as
Par art mei ne decevras pas.

656 Tos les deus jur que jeo aour
Que morir te ferai a dolor,
Se tu mun deu plus tost n'aoures,
De sacrefisse ne l'honores.'

660 Saint Lorenz dit: 'Torment ne dot,

635 maitre

Tei et ton deu guerpis del tot.
Quanque faire veus, tost le fai.
El nun Jesus le recevrai.'
664   Decius l'ot, mult est iriez.
Idunc l'unt tost despoillez,
De *plunbatis* l'unt debatu.
Dirai vos quel torment ceo fu:
668   Unes coroies qui sunt quarees,
A clous de plun soudé plummees.
D'icest le batent asprement,
N'a menbre qui ne soit tot samglent.
672   Par tot le cors lui funt granz plaies,
Parfundes, horibles et laies.
La ou il est si angoissous $6^r b$
Dunc dist: 'Damnedeu glorious,
676   Sire, receif mon esperit.'
Dunt oent une vois del ciel qui dit:
'Greignor estrif te sunt deu
Que tu n'en as encore eu.'
680   Et Decius la voiz entent;
Dunt dit: 'Ohi, romaine gent,
Oez cum la voiz del deable
Conforte ici cest mescreable.
684   Il ne dote ne deu ne mei,
Ne il ne crient prince ne rei;
Tant par est plain d'enchantemenz
Ne crient maus, ne tormenz.
688   Pernez le mei, sel me batez,
De toz tormenz le tormentez!'
Romain l'unt dunc agraventé
En un leu *catasta* nunmé.
692   Ceo ert un leu ou l'en soloit
Metre les chetis en destreit.
Iloc lui funt torment mult grant.
Dunc dit le saint en soriant:
696   'Damnedeu Pere en qui jeo crei,
Sire, aies merci de mei!

666 Et de plunbaus

Conforte ton serf par ta grace,
E si que cist poples le sace
700 Que tu es Deus, tot pues sauver
Et bon confort a ceus doner
Qui en cest ciecle por t'amor
Sofrirunt mal, peine et dolor.
704 Aies de ton serf remenbrance;
Si demostre ta grant poissance!'
Tresque out dit ceste oroison   6va
Uns paens, Romanus out non,
708 Saut avant, a ses piés chai,
Dit lui: 'Aies merci de mi!
En Jesu Crist le tuen Deu crei;
Car jeo vei ester devant tei
712 Un jovencel a un drap blanc
Qui de tes plaies tert le sanc.
Baptisez mei, por Deu amor,
El nun Jesu, tun Creator,
716 Qui te deigna revisiter
Par son angre, et conforter
En cest peril, en cest torment.'
Decius dit quant il l'entent
720 A Valerien qui iloc fu:
'Trai sunmes et deceu
Par art et par enchantement!'
Dunc a conmandé a sa gent
724 Deslier lei de *catasta*;
Quant osté fu, sel conmanda
A Ypolite por garder,
Mais del paleis nel deit mener.
728 Et Romanus prent un cruçun;
Plain de eve l'aporte al barun,
E prie lui qu'il le baptist
El nun son Seignor Jesu Crist.
732 Et saint Lorenz l'eve receit,
Prinseigné l'a et beneit,
Dunc le baptiz[e] el nun Jesu.

724 del castata

Quant Decius l'a entendu
736 Devant lui le fait tost venir,
Car sa creance veut oir.
Ains que nul riens lui demant
En halt crie et dit al tirant:
740 'Jeo sui crestiens, merci Dé.'
Mainent lei defors la cité.
A une porte que iloc aveit,
Salaria nunmee esteit,
744 La lui coupent por Deu la teste.
Encore gardent cel jor la feste
En aaust la quinte kalende.
Deus por s'amor gueredon rende
748 A ceus qui gardent cel jor,
Ou qui por Deu lui funt honor.
Aprés ceo que decolez fu,
Nuitantre est por le cors venu
752 Justinus, qui prestre esteit,
Que saint Sixte ordené aveit.
En une crote l'unt enterré;
Grant obsequie i ont celebré.

756   Cist est mors cum bons crestiens.
Decius et Valeriens
Vunt cele noit conseiller
Cum peussent saint Lorenz traiter.
760 Tot dreit vunt del temple Jovis
As termes Olimpiadis.
Termes en Rome ceo est uns leus
Ou paens soulent faire gieus.
764 Passent par le theatre Auguste
Dejoste le palais Saluste.
Son tribunal i fait drecier;
Siet i et tuit si chevaler.
768 En cele nuit a conmandé
Que saint Lorenz soit amené.

6^{v}b

751 nuitrante   761 terines

Ypolitus en a tristor,   7^{r}a
De pité plore et de tendror.
772   Lorenz dit: 'Ne plorer, amis,
Mais tais tei et si te esjois.
Car la ou vois, arai vitoire;
El ciel m'est aprestee gloire,
776   Lasus ou li archangre sunt.'
Ypolitus al saint respunt:
'Crestiens sui, en Jesu crei;
Et por que ne vois dunc o tei?
780   Por quei ne vois o tei morir,
Car a la gloire voil partir?'
'Or del sofrir,' dit saint Lorenz:
'Ceile Deu en ton cuer laenz;
784   Mais tresque manderai por tei
Si oi ma voiz et vien a mei!'

Decius, plain de ire et de mal
Se siet en son sié tribunal.
788   Por saint Lorenz espoenter
Et por sa gloire destorber,
Fait demostrer toz ses tormenz
En la veue de ses genz.
792   Li torment erent si hisdous
Et a nonmer si merveillous
Que n'est huem qui en char vive,
Ne jeo ne altre, ques descrive.
796   Quant Decius vit les tormenz
Par ire dit a saint Lorenz:
'Guerpis l'engin de artimage
Et si me di tost ton parage.'
800   Saint Lorenz dit: 'Espaneis sui;
Des enfance ci nori fui.
Baptesme reçui en m'esfance,   7^{r}b
En Jesu Crist ai ma fiance.
804   Gramaire apris et letreure,
Estoires et altre escripture;
Et ma jovente et mon eé
Ai tot mis en divinité.'

808 Et Decius dit: 'Vairement
    Devins es par enchantement!
    Tant sés de la devine lei
    Que tu ne criens ne deu, ne mei,
812 Peril ne peine, ne angoisse,
    Ne torment que faire te poisse.'
    Saint Lorenz respunt al tirant:
    'En Deu le mien Pere crei tant
816 Que jeo ne criem nule faisance
    Que soit encontre ma creance.'
    Decius en est mult dolenz.
    De pieres le fait batre es denz,
820 Et dit: 'Male nuit est venue,
    En tei iert tote despendue,
    En peine, en peris, en tormenz.'
    Idunc lui respunt saint Lorenz:
824 'En ma noit n'a point de oscurté,
    Mes tote reluist en clarté.'
    Cele male gent mescreue
    La bouche li unt rebatue.
828 Saint Lorenz se rest confortez
    Et dit dunc: 'Deu en soit loez!
    Jesu Crist, a tei graces rent,
    Car tu es Deu omnipotent.'
832 Dunc dit Decius: 'Cha donez
    Un lit de fer ou seit posez
    Lorenz, li orguellous hardiz.' $7^v a$
    Devant lui est porté uns liz
836 Qui fu fait cumme gerdis de fers;
    Treis bares i out en travers.
    Devant Decium l'unt asis;
    Saint Lorenz ont nu desus mis.
840 Dunc i aportent li serjant
    En paeles charbun ardant;
    Sos le greil les esparpeillent,
    Saint Lorenz rostent et greellent.
844 Decius desvez al saint dit
    Que il a ses deus sacrefit.
    Saint Lorenz dit al cuvert:

'Mei ai en sacrefise osfert
848   A Deu, a qui sui donez,
Car esperit qu'est atriblez
Est sacrefise al Creator.'
Ici entendi a l'autor,
852   Al prophete Davi qui dit:
'Quer atriblé Deu ne despit.'

Saint Lorenz gist sus le greil;
De totes pars lui funt peril.
856   Li serjant ventent le charbun;
Esparpeillent lei sos le barun.
De forches de fer qu'il tenoient
Cuntre le greil son cors premoient.
860   A Decium dist saint Lorenz:
'Ore poez veer, chetif, dolenz,
Que ti charbun me sunt frigerie
Et a tei torment et miserie.
864   Deu set bien quant acusé fui
Nel neai, cumme Deu le conui,
Et demandez le regei.
Ore sui ars, lui en rent merci!'

7^{v}b

868   Sus le greil, la ou il gist
En rent merci a Jesu Crist.
A cest vers a bien entendu:
'Passames par eve et par fu,
872   En refrigerie nos menas,
A tei en rendun *gratias*.'
Valerien qui prevost fu
Dit al saint: 'Ou sunt li fu
876   Que tu a nos deus prametoies
Quant deis que tu les ardroies?'
Et sain Lorenz dunc lui respunt
Et dit as princes qui iloc sunt:
880   'Ohi, chetif maleuré
De desverie forsené!
Et n'avés vos dunc entendu
Que nule ardor n'ai d'icest fu?

884   Ne jeo nel sent n'en char, n'en os,
        Ains m'est frigerie et repos.'
        Tuit icil qui iloc esteient,
        Hisdor et grant pité aveient
888   De la crualté Decii
        Qui vif le fait rostir issi.
        Dunc dist saint Lorenz en riant
        O simple vult, o bel semblant:
892   'Deu, tei en puisse jeo loer
        Qui ci me deignas conforter.'
        Ovre les oils et dunc si dit
        Decio que devant lui vit:
896   'Chaitif, l'altre part car tornez;
        Mangez deça, quit est assez!'
        Gloire et grace a Deu en rent $8^r a$
        Et dit: 'Pater Omnipotent,
900   Jesu Crist, a tei graces rent,
        Qui m'as doné ceste memoire
        Que envers tei deservi ai,
        Si qu'a tes portes entrerai.'
904   Et li sains cum out ceo dit
        A Deu tramet son esperit.
        Dreit al ciel vait l'alme del saint.
        Le cors sus le greil remaint.

908   Quant Decius out iceo fait,
        O le prevost d'iloc s'en vait.
        El paleis Tiberii s'en vunt,
        Le cors saint Lorenz laissé ont.
912   Ypolite, ains qu'il fust jor,
        L'en a porté o grant douçor.
        Les oilz li clot, les piés li juint
        Et d'aromat trestuit l'enuint;
916   En un drap l'a envolepé.
        A saint Justin l'a puis mandé,
        Cum Decius alez esteit,
        Cum le cors lessé aveit

913 honor *expuncted*   914 p. li puint

920 Sus le gredil, sus le charbun.
 Justinus vint al barun
 Plorant et triste et dolenz.
 Enportent le cors saint Lorenz;
924 *In Tiburtina* l'unt porté
 Si l'unt tresque a la nuit gardé.
 En une croute l'enterrerent
 Que en Tiburtina troverent.
928 *In agro Verano*, el pré,
 Qui ert *illius vidue*,
 A qui saint Lorenz out rendu,
 Devant ceo, santé et salu.   *8^{r}b*
932 Iloc l'unt bel enseveli
 Ens en la quarte ide *augusti*.
 Treis jors firent jeunesons,
 Vegiles et afliciuns.
936 Plorerent et furent dolent
 Tote la crestiene gent.
 Justinus la messe chanta;
 Corpus Cristi a toz dona,
940 En l'onor Deu et sa memoire.
 Prium lui qu'il nos doinst gloire,
 Ou regne en joie parmanable,
 Ke por fait dunt soion copable
944 Ne aillum en peril, ne en peine,
 Ne perdun joie soveraine,
 Mais faire nos doinst tel faisance
 Que aveir puissun sostenance,
948 Et la gloire de parais,
 Jesu, la ou regnes et vis. Amen.

942 eu r. 946 tele

VARIANT READINGS OF MS. *B*
(London, B.M. Egerton 2710)

Incipit co est la uie sein lorenz ki pur dev suffri turmenz   2 cum a d.
3 de cel e.   4 s. dist   6 e. ami v.   10 ne enemi en   11 lure de m.
12 e. del m.   13 ami a b.   14 e enemi al m. se couere   18 t. matire
19 me perceif   20 s. fors un   23 q. vus d.   27 chescvn deit eschire la
31 nen reveve   38 d. v est o.   39 g. sens aristotles   40 r. danz c.
47 *and* 48 *are interverted in B*   47 n. e a n. revet   50 m. e p.
51 s. cum li   57 dalcvn o.   59 en *not in B*   62 qui p.
65 ore p.; p. sa a.   67 f. tel o.   68 a. neient p.   73 sa seinte m.
75 cest ouere face q. ci comence   76 p. un ancel sein lorence
77 se estorie   80 bon *not in B*; v. atendre   83 d. aura e sa
84 si cvme l.   85 d. bon ouere s.   88 li hom e.   89 deables p. lur c.
90 evrent e.   92 pur ces q.   98 ore v.   99 sa cruelte quilvertisse
100 d. seint eglise   101 premier *not in B*   102 a. volt e.
106 tres *not in B*   107 il *not in B*; a. ad t.   109 les sulur s.
113 f. seez en   117 vent sur   123 vos *not in B*   129 q. tut l.
130 d. cesar neit ia   134 q. frai kar mamenez
135 q. frai ici; jeo *not in B*   136 s. lur r.   138 s. tresqual t.
139 ne me g.; me siueras   141 f. de cest d.   142 m. vist
143 m. dust   150 et *not in B*   154 s. lentendi   161 p. amur de
162 a. que li   168 se p.   172 nos *not in B*   173 oil io t.
175 a deu fras   178 s. tut d.   183 dune s.   188 aiez m.; t. age
190 ne metre; *first* ne *not in B*   191 que mal e.
198 t. come io s. de greignur age   199 t. deigne deus melz s.
200 e la l.   201 que nuls   203 d. co e.   204 d. comanda a
205 m. lever   207 li comanda a   208 d. li meinent
209 a sun ymage   210 *not in B*   211 ymage *not in B*   213 d. seie e
216 li chevalers c.   218 et *not in B*   219 m. li s.
220 l. vint si lateint   221 q. frai   222 t. despendv ai   223 d. lai d.
226 ne fuisse a   228 p. lunt s.   229 il reconuit   230 p. done lut
231 f. le g.   234 c. qui od   244 c. de capitolie   245 l. li d.
246 le tresor a.   251 ki lur tresor ad   254 quil mameine t.
257 m. liez le   258 e a d.   259 se esleca   260 le tresor
262 l. ren ne   266 liuerer   275 menat le   277 grant *not in B*
278 que f.   280 g. tens i; ja *not in B*   281 co quil fu
282 ne v. de li i. fere   286 e dico qui tant lunt r.   287 q. ren ne vit
290 d. li dit s.   291 c. voleit   292 il crerra melz   293 d. que v.
303 la renome p.   304 c. e v.   305 e paraliti   306 langvissant j.
308 grant *not in B*   310 r. les g.   312 toz *not in B*
313 loez s. deus e   314 e nos; tele   318 lum auera delit. amen
321 m. od les v.   323 c. si d.   325 i. li d.   327 t. li mustera

328 p. auera   329 y. co oi   330 tost *not in B*   332 j. frai co
337 t. se turne   338 m. de m.   342 lui *not in B*
343 le ewangelie d.   348 v dev a   349 vos *not in B*   352 kal ure v.
356 cume bel r.   358 mult tost *expuncted after* corage *in B*
363 *two lines in B*: sain lorenz a lui dit / creies tu en iesv crist
364 y. li dit   365 e p.   366 e quil resceint s. espirit   371 sa mesne
372 t. baptize   373 tuit p.   375 la doctrine
380 l. sun nun p. amen   384 a sa c.   385 e li d.   387 d. est c.
388 d. li s.   390 o. tresqua l.   391 sa mesne   392 e. aparille
398 qui l.   399 d. ore me   401 v. dit e o.   402 tei s. come
406 il pout t.   407 t. sunt d.   409 musce les ad en sa m.
412 s. el siez l.   413 le b.   415 quand *not in B*; sain l.
416 g. quil o.   417 e dist t. oant   418 veez ci le t. que ja ne
420 tel e.   422 d. en e.   426 n. frun de   432 aure d. cum p.
433 nest l.   434 d. que e.   436 s. et mu   437 seint e. yles les
439 ore s.   441 que home f. u co que f.   443 que home
445 que home   451 car *not in B*; ceo *not in B*   453 p. halt q.
454 u o.; c. que home f.   455 m. un f.   456 c. tot o.
457 f. en s.; de *not in B*   460 tresquil s.   462 kar t. c. pur co; il dit
465 tot *not in B*   470 enfern et   477 la virgine d.
484 n. redempcinn   486 *neither* de *in B*   487 nus fu v.
494 d. le premer fruz   495 d. cist en   496 f. tut p.
499 fumes tut d.   503 c. dume   505 si vivera   507 u tu i.
512 l. el cel el s.   515 jo tenc p.   523 lei *not in B*   524 c. li f.
527 g. en r.   530 s. sersf me   531 j. rei p.   536 ne fra
538 fait *not in B*   541 de fuz de fers de   546 ci aportez
547 tu serras en   549 ta fol e. lesser   550 l. dit al turmentur
551 le men a.   555 que d.   556 d. li d.   557 t' *not in B*
559 c. le r.   560 s. enseignez l.   561 frai l.   565 de tels v.
566 de tels t.   567 lur n.   568 escrit en   570 lier le; m. a lui
576 il unt f.   578, 579 *not in B*   580 d. les ta   583 c. frai j.
584 ne te fiez t.   585 que lum aljun metrum t.   586 i. tes tresors si
587 que c.   588 eschive les t.   591 quil n.   594 g. errur e siu la
595 e sacrefise a   596 ne quidez p.   597 p. cuntre m.
605 en lui m.   608 c. el t.   610 ja pur n.   611 tot *not in B*
612 deus m.   613 f. poz o.   617 g. colps d.   619 g. te r.
621 e. dicele quapres aurai   622 t. ore poez uer   627 d. escrie e
628 denchantement   629 pur co   630 ore aueras   631 f. porter l.
632 co ert m.   637 e bruille q.   638 les coste e
639 c. li bruille desqual os   640 dit lorenz dev v.   641 aie s.
646 es jhesu v.   654 tu *not in B*   655 deceveras; pas *not in B*
657 te frai a   659 s. ne h.   660 s. lorent d.   661 d. guerpi del
662 le frai   663 le receverai   665 t. despuille   667 v. de q.
668 c. que s.   669 as chefs de   671 m. que ne; tot *not in B*
672 c. li f. grant p.   676 s. receis m.   678 s. du   682 v. al d.
683 c. ci c.   685 c. ne p.   686 denchantement   687 ne turment
691 l. castalla n.   692 u home s.   693 chetifs endreit   694 i. li f.

695 d. li s.   697 s. eez m.   699 issi q. cest pople s.   700 t. poez s.
702 p. ta a.   703 sofrent m.   706 d. cest o.   707 un paen r.
709 d. lut; de mei   710 le ton d.   713 p. tret le   718 en t.
724 d. le de castalla   731 n. nostre s.   736 d. li le   738 n. ren l.
741 m. le fors de la   742 p. quiloc a.   743 s. nume e.   744 la li c.
745 vncore lui gardent cil j.   747 dev p.   749 qui *not in B*
750 q. decole fu   753 o. esteit; aveit *written above* esteit
754 c. lad e.   759 cume puisent s.   761 as termis o.   762 t. e r.
763 p. soleint f.   764 le chartre a.   767 t. li c.   769 l. i s. mene
772 ne plurez a.   773 et *not in B*; te jois   774 v. aurai v.
775 en c.; apreste g.   779, 780 *are combined in B*: e pur quei ne vois
dunc murir od tei   782 ore d.   785 oez ma v. si venez a
786 p. dire e   788 l. esponter   792 le t. ert si
795 a. quis puisse descrivre   798 e. dartimage   800 l. dist e.
801 n. sui   804 recvi *expuncted before* apris; e lettrure
811 ne d. ne rei   813 te *not in B*   815 le men p. en c.
816 ne dut n.   819 des p.; b. as d.   820 n. te e.   822 en peril en
823 i. li r.   824 p. doscvrte   827 b. lui v.   828 r. conforte
829 s. loe   831 car *not in B*; es devs o.   832 ca venez;
portez *written above* venez   833 f. v il s.   834 l. lorgoillus
835 p. un liz   836 que fu; gredilz   839 nu *not in B*
840 i portent li   841 p. carbuns a.   842 les esparpeillerent
846 al *not in B*   849 e. qui e.   852 al prophese d.   856 v. li c.
857 sparpeillent desuz le   860 d. dit s.   862 s. refrigerie
864 decius s.; q. accusez f.   869 graces rend a j.   873 r. graces
875 dist al; li feu   877 les ardereies   878 d. li r.   879 p. que i.
883 q. nul ardv nai de cest fev   884 s. en c.   886 i. quilevc e.
890 d. dit s.; en oant   891 s. voiz od   892 devs en p.
893 que ci me deignastes visiter; conforter *written above* visiter
894 si dist   895 d. qui d.   898 e graces a   900 g. en r.
902 qui vers t.   904 li seint c.   910 s' *not in B*   912 il fu j.
914 o. lui c.; p. lui puint   917 p. comande   918 come d. ale e.
919 e cum   922 ploranz tristes e d.   932 l. ben e.
933 ens *not in B*   934 trei j. f. juneisuns   936 plurent e
940 d. en sa   941 preum nus q.   944 nalium en p. en p.
947 p. sa s.

NOTES

1. W. Söderhjelm (*De saint Laurent*, pp. xiv, xxxiii), and Gaston Paris (*Romania* XVII (1888), 610—12) have noted the similarity of the opening lines of *St. Laurent* with the following lines from the *Cumpoz* of Philippe de Thaon (ed. E. Mall, Strasbourg, 1873):

> Maistre, or vus esdreciez,
> A cest busuin m'aidiez!
> Suvienget vus que dit
> Li vilains par respit:
> Al busuin est truvez
> L'amis e espruvez.
> Unkes ne fut ami
> Ki al busuin failli,
> Dunt il poüst aidier
> Ne de rien cunseillier.
> Pur çol di, ne targiez.
> Mais ma raisun oïez;
> Pri vus de l'esculter
> E puis de l'amender;
> Kar or voil cumencier
> Iço dunt voil traitier,
> E chapitles poser,
> Ses volez amender.
> Volez le, bien le sai;
> Or les i poserai.
>
> (ll. 161—180)

3. **Sovienge vus** 'May you be reminded', 'Remember'.

4. Cf. Ecclesiasticus 12:8—9, Proverbs 7:17. For similar proverbs in O.F. see Le Roux de Lincy, *Livre des proverbes français* (Paris, 1859), II, 231—232, 473. Jesus the son of Sirach who lived about 200 years before Christ was the author of Ecclesiasticus. This latter work, first written in Hebrew, was later translated into Greek by another Jesus, the grandson of the author.

12. **l'enpeint de munt el val** Cf. M. Wilmotte's translation: 'le fait tomber de haut en bas', *Le Moyen Age* II (1889), 6.

14. **coivre** A spelling variant for O.F. *cuevre*. MS. *B* has *covere*.

29. A citation from Ecclesiastes on vanity. The opening line of Eccl. says it is written by the son of David. Cf. Eccl. 1:10 for ll. 31, 32.

31. Although T.-L. and Gdfr. give no examples of such usage, *renueve* seems to be used intransitively here, 'nothing renews itself'.

33—34. 'No one can have such wealth that another has not had just such wealth (before).' i.e. there is no opulence that a previous generation has not already matched. This theme is expanded in ll. 35—37. *A*'s *autel* 34 has been corrected on the basis of *B*.

35. The reading in *B* is superior.

43. The missing word has been supplied from MS. *B*.

48. The reference is to worldly pursuits. Lines 47 and 48 are in reverse order in *B*, which perhaps makes the sense clearer.

52. que qu'il demuert 'however much it delays', i.e. however long it is delayed, both the rich man and the poor man come to one (and the same) thing — death.

54—58. 'I see nothing enduring in this world except this, that a person does good for which he may have mercy after his death, or receive praise or fame for some work which remains after him in this world.'

75—76. The work has been commissioned by *une ancele saint Lorenz*. As M. D. Legge points out, the word *ancele* (also used by the Nun of Barking with reference to herself, cf. Södergård, l. 530) 'was used, like *ancilla*, for nun as well as servant. . . . And this suggests that the patroness was a nun, probably an abbess or prioress, of a convent dedicated to St. Lawrence.' Miss Legge further suggests that 'it may be possible that one of the twelfth-century prioresses [of the convent at Oldbury, Warwickshire] was a patroness of literature, and caused to be written not only the Life of St. Lawrence but those of St. Modwenna and St. Osyth also.' See *Anglo-Norman Literature and its Background* (Oxford, 1963), p. 251.

77. s'estoire The rejected reading, *se estoire*, found in both manuscripts, is probably a scribal repetition of the letter.

84. This line is no doubt a reference to the Latin source used by the author. See Sources, above.

85. The variant in *B*, *bon overe*, allows 'correct' scansion, although the meaning of *A* is more plausible. Söderhjelm counts *beneuré* as three syllables.

87. 'The greater part of the world was pagan territory.'

93—94. These details are found only in the abridged Latin sources. See Sources, above.

95. Decius Cesar The Latin hagiography, dating from around the end of the fifth century, has attributed the persecution of Sixtus and Lawrence to Decius, Roman emperor A.D. 249—51, rather than to Valerian, emperor A.D. 253—259/60. The legend has in fact confused the two completely: as an article in the *New Catholic Encyclopedia* (New York, 1967) states, 'so strong was the impression made on Christians by the persecution of Decius that in later times martyrdoms about which little or nothing was known were described in terms of the persecution of Decius' (vol. 4, 701). Such is the case with *St. Laurent*; it was Decius who in A.D. 250 ordered the Christians 'to appear before special commissions and perform some act of public worship to the Roman gods' (loc. cit.). As Delehaye points out in his article on the legend (*Analecta Bollandiana* LI (1933), 34—72), the edict of Valerian in August A.D. 258 ordered the summary execution of

bishops, priests, and deacons upon their identification as such (pp. 43–44). Sixtus was surprised and executed in a cemetery where he was preaching to the faithful; the manner of Lawrence's death several days later is unknown, but it was probably by the sword (pp. 49–50). The scenes between Sixtus and Lawrence concerning the treasure of the Church, and the subsequent interrogation and torture of Lawrence on the grill have no historical basis. The probable eastern origin of this part of the legend is discussed by Delehaye in the article mentioned above.

96–102. The first part of the longer Latin legend, of which the martyrdom of Sixtus and Lawrence is the central episode, takes place in Persia. Decius, during a successful campaign in the east, captured Babylon and executed the bishop Polychronius, as part of his general persecution of the Christians. According to legend, Decius later brought back to Rome the two Christian princes, Abdon and Sennen, who were martyred before Sixtus. The hagiographer has confused Decius, who did not campaign in the east, with Valerian, who did (although unsuccessfully: he was captured by the Persian king Sapor in 259 and died in captivity in 260). See Delehaye, op. cit., pp. 36–37, and *The New Catholic Encyclopedia* (New York, 1967), vol. 14, 520.

117. **vient** The rejected form is corrected on the basis of *B*.

132–40. The Anglo-Norman author introduces at this point in the narrative only the beginning of a long and eloquent speech by Lawrence to Sixtus found in the Latin versions: *Quo progrederis sine filio, pater? quo, sacerdos sancte, sine diacono properas? . . . (P.P.*, section 13; see Sources, above). The reply by Sixtus is also shortened from the Latin: *Non ego te, fili, desero, neque derelinquo . . . Post venies; flere desiste; post triduum sequeris sacerdotem levita (P.P.*, section 13). The Latin confirms the reading of *A*, l. 139, as opposed to that of *B*.

142. The superior reading from *B* has been adopted.

150. Although the meaning is a little obscure, the fact that the treasure was *sold* is found in the abridged Latin sources: *Tunc beatus Laurentius omnia quae perceperat christianis artificibus vendidit et omne pretium pauperibus erogavit* (see Sources, above). Söderhjelm suggests that the line means the treasure was sold to Christian goldsmiths.

153. 'He paid back His (God's) blessing.'

156–7. Cf. Psalms 112:9.

164. The reading of *B*, which avoids the repetition of *fust* in rhyme, has been adopted.

169. **sunt** from *B*.

175. The line has been corrected on the basis of the reference to the gods in the plural in ll. 179 ff. and the plural pronoun adopted from *B* in l. 177.

176. The adopted reading is found in *B*.

190. The original probably had a single *ne* as in *B* (giving a metrically 'correct' line), with the subj. pr. *metes* co-ordinated with *muerges*; but *B* has introduced the infin. used as a negative imperative (see Syntax, 6, above).

192. The conjunction 'if' seems to be missing; perhaps *Crei ceo ke* (also in *B*) is for an original *Crei ke se.*

211. The correction is based on *B*.

217. The adopted reading is found in *B*.

219—226. The Anglo-Norman author here returns to Lawrence's long speech to Sixtus, from which he had borrowed earlier (ll. 132-40), in addition to following his source, which at this point has only: *noli me derelinquere, pater sancte, quia iam thesauros expendi, quos tradidisti mihi* (*P.P.*, section 18). ll. 225—26 have their Latin equivalent in section 13 of the *P.P.* version: *Tu numquam sacrificasti sine ministro nec offerre consueveras*. The meaning of the Anglo-Norman is: 'When were you (ever) in the habit of making sacrifice that I was not at your service (i.e. without my being at your service)?'

220. The rejected form *atant* is probably a scribal slip.

231. lei For this form of the masc. sg. direct object pronoun (which seems to be peculiar to MS. *A* of *St. Laurent*) see Morphology, B, above.

239—40. In the Latin sources Sixtus and the deacons are interred in different cemeteries.

251. lors tresors The *-s* of *lors* (*lur* in *B*) is perhaps due to a scribal anticipation of the ending of *tresors* rather than an early analogical form (Mod. F. *leurs*).

254. The original line probably ran *Et di lui qu'il le m'amaint tost*, differently altered by the two scribes.

258. The original no doubt had *Decio*, dative, as at ll. 403, 895, without the preposition *a* introduced by both scribes.

260. The correction to *les tresors* (against the sg. in both manuscripts) is supported not only by the plural verb in 261, but also by the use of the pl. in other passages (see ll. 222—3, 229—30, 251, 324—27, 398—400, 407); it was suggested by G. Paris and M. Wilmotte in their reviews of Söderhjelm's edition.

267. prevost The Latin title is *praefectus (urbis)*. The legend makes Valerian a chief subordinate of Decius. See above, note on l. 95.

273. vicaire From the Latin *vicarium*; Hippolytus's position is that of chief subaltern to Valerian. The character of Hippolytus as found in the Latin legend used as a source here is historically inaccurate; cf. Delehaye, op. cit., pp. 58 ff.

314. The original must have had the phonetic fem. form *tel* as in l. 946 in *B*.

344. Cf. Romans 8:31.

345. 'He . . . has little cause to be worried.' The subject of *puet* is the impersonal subject that goes with *chaleir*.

349—53. Cf. Matt. 10:18—19; Mark 13:9—11; Luke 21:12—15.

363. This hypermetrical line is made two lines in *B*. Söderhjelm drops *tu* from the line. The scene has been expanded by the Anglo-Norman author with details borrowed from the Latin source describing Lucillus' baptism in the previous section.

377. avant 'further on'. This is a reference to the part of the legend

following Lawrence's burial, dealing with the martyrdoms of Hippolytus and his household. The Anglo-Norman author of *St. Laurent* does not fulfil this promise in the poem as we know it. This use of *avant* is found in *Le Besant de Dieu*; see the edition by P. Ruelle (Brussels, 1973), l. 87 and note.

403. The correct form is supplied by *B*.

418. The correct form is found in *B*.

440. The correction is based on *B*, and the Latin source, which reads: *vos ipsi iudicate, quis debet adorari, qui factus est vel qui fecit* (*P.P.*, section 22).

441. 'That which man makes, or He who made them (men)?' The original must have had the nom. form *(h)om* at ll. 441, 443, 445.

443. **Qui** Written at the beginning of the following line in the manuscript, this word is needed as the rhyme word of 443. The corresponding text in the Latin for 442–3 is: *Decius Caesar dixit: 'Quis factus est vel quis fecit?'* (*P.P.*, section 22).

444–515. The long development on the distinction between *creature* and *faiture* is launched from a paraphrase of the short reply made to the question posed by Decius in the Latin version, cited above. The Latin reads: *Beatus Laurentius dixit: Deus, pater domini nostri Jesu Christi, creator est omnis creaturae, hominum et volucrum et pecorum et bestiarum et iumentorum et piscium et coeli et terrae. Et tu dicis: sacrificia lapidibus et adora facturas surdas et mutas?* (*P.P.*, section 22).

448–50. '(God's) Creation should not, according to reason, worship that which is (man) made, nor dishonour its Creator.'

451–53. There is probably a line or lines missing preceding 451, which remains without a rhyming line. The subject of *aore* is *creature*, unstated: 'For when it (Creation) worships that which man makes it demeans itself, for Creation is nobler than the work of man.'

454. 'That which man makes is (remains merely) the work of a particular man.'

473. **estreine** The rejected reading is no doubt a scribal reversal of letters.

479. **Creator**, as nom., may here be intended to be Latin; elsewhere the form *creator* (*creatur* in *B*) is used only as acc., and the nom. is *crieres* 468.

486–87. The two lines seem to require a verb such as *vint* rather than *fu* 487, particularly since *fu* is used again in ll. 489, 490, 491. The variant in *B* 486 makes the use of *fu* in 487 more grammatically acceptable, although *B* 486 is not octosyllabic. It is possible that the model used by the scribes of *A* and *B* was faulty, and was corrected by *B*, not by *A*.

496–97. The same word, *fust*, is used for both the Tree of Knowledge with its forbidden fruit, and the Tree of the Cross. This contrast is a medieval commonplace (see M. D. Legge, *Anglo-Norman Literature*, p. 252).

536. **el** This is the only instance of this neuter pronoun in the text, used with the meaning 'anything (different)', i.e. the present torture is without effect.

537. halt Lawrence has been beaten while in a prostrate position and now is raised to his feet again. (The Latin here reads: *Decius Caesar dixit: Levate eum a terra et date ante conspectum eius omne genus tormentorum, P.P.*, section 23.)

542—43. 'There was no (instrument of) torture ever made which he (Decius) did not display before the faithful one of God (Lawrence).'

547. ieres The original must have had *iers* (cf. *B*'s *serras*); similarly *ier* 554 where both *A* and *B* have *iere*. For fut. forms of *estre* with final *-e* see Explicative Note on *Horn* 45.

550. MS. *B* has the verb stated, *S. Lorenz dit al turmentur*, as it usually is in this construction in the poem.

556—62. In this ironical question addressed to Lawrence, Decius uses the Christian terms of defection, *escumengé* and *renoié*, to refer to those who have left the Roman gods and become Christians.

585. This line, which is corrupt in *B*, has no equivalent in the Latin, which reads: *Declara nobis omnes profanos ut mundetur civitas; et tu ipse sacrifica diis et noli confidere in thesauris quos absconditos habes (P.P.,* section 24).

594. lei The imperative of *laier* (cf. 580). The original probably had this form rather than the reading in *B: e siu la lei.* See Phonology, above.

631. laminas The Latin word is explained in the vernacular in the lines that follow. The source text reads: *Decius Caesar dixit: 'Fustibus augete, et date ad latera eius lamminas ferreas ardentes' (P.P.,* section 24).

645. The line is not directly borrowed from the source, which reads: *... interrogatus te dominum (Jesum Christum* is a variant) *confessus sum (P.P.,* section 24).

666. plunbatis Once again the author explains the nature of the instrument of torture in the vernacular.

673. laies For this fem. form see Phonology, 11, above.

691. catasta The Latin word is spelled correctly here in *A*, as opposed to *castata* 724. In *B*, the word appears as *castalla* in both instances. *Nunmé* here means 'called (in Latin)', rather than indicating a proper name.

707. Uns paens Romanus is a soldier in the Latin source: *unus de militibus (P.P.,* section 26).

724. catasta Cf. note on 691 above.

746. The fifth Calend of August is July 28 in the modern calendar.

751. Nuitantre The rejected form *nuitrante* of *A* is cited by Gdfr. from this text only.

761. termes The reading of *B*, *termis*, may be intended as the Latin ablative *T(h)ermis*; but in 762 both manuscripts have the vernacular *termes*.

779—80. The two lines are combined in *B* into one hypermetric line.

782. Or del sofrir 'Be patient', 'resign yourself'; cf. Syntax, 6, above.

794—95. The Anglo-Norman writer, by the poetic exaggeration of these two lines, excuses himself from describing these instruments of torture (in contrast to the earlier explanation of *laminas* and *plunbatis*). The Latin list reads: *Plumbatas, fustes, lamminas, ungues, lectos, batilos (P.P.,* section 27).

820. The reading in *B* is perhaps more likely to be the original.

836. gerdis This form in *A* (*B* has *gredilz*) is the nom. sg. of *gerdil*, which must have arisen by metathesis from *gredil* (so in both manuscripts at 920) at a time when this still had an intervocalic dental consonant; cf. Pope §1177). There may be a connection with Northern Eng. *girdle*, metathetic form of *griddle*.

847. The use of *aveir* with reflexive verbs is found in Anglo-Norman, and, more rarely, in other dialects. See P. Ménard, *Syntaxe de l'ancien français* (2nd ed., Bordeaux, 1973), §127 (b).

849–50 and 853. Cf. Psalms 51:17.

866. Et demandez le regei 'And when questioned I confessed Him' (cf. 644).

871–73. These lines are similar to the version found in the Oxford Psalter: *Nus trespassames par fu e par ewe, e forsmenas nus en refrigerie* (*Libri Psalmorum Versio Antiqua Gallica*, ed. Franciscus Michel, Oxford, 1860, Ps. 65:11, p. 84).

891. vult The reading of *A* is supported by the Latin which reads: *ille autem vultu placido dicebat* (*P.P.*, section 28).

896–905. The Latin source here reads: '*Ecce, miser, assasti tibi partem unam; regira aliam et manduca.*' *Tunc gratias agens Deo cum gloria dixit: 'Gratias tibi ago, domine Jesu Christe, quia merui ianuas tuas ingredi.' Et statim emisit spiritum* (*P.P.*, section 28). Lines 898–900 all have the same rhyme, while l. 901 remains without a rhyme. Söderhjelm counted a missing line after 901; H. Suchier, in his review, proposed to solve the problem by correcting 900 to read: ... *a tei rend la gloire*. If the Anglo-Norman writer was following the Latin source closely, Suchier's solution may be the correct one. One could also speculate that two lines have fallen out from the original, one rhyming with 900 and one with 901.

914. juint This correction, first suggested by G. Paris in his review of the 1888 edition, seems demanded by the sense. The body is being laid out in a dignified position for burial.

922. The original may have had, as *B* does, the forms *ploranz* and *tristes*, in apposition with *Justinus* 921, although the Latin reads: *Tunc beatus Justinus presbyter et Yppolitus plorantes et multum tristes tulerunt ...* (*P.P.*, section 29). There is no direct statement in the Latin, however, for l. 921, so it is possible that the Anglo-Norman writer chose to make l. 922 refer to the arrival of Justinus, rather than to the removal of the body.

929. illius vidue A Latin possessive genitive (the widow who owned the burial site was one Cyriaca, whom Lawrence had earlier healed). The Anglo-Norman writer has also used Latin phrases to refer to the other indications of place connected with the burial site, ll. 924, 928.

930–31. These lines are the only reference to the earlier part of the legend, omitted by our author, in which Lawrence heals various Christians after he has distributed the wealth of the Church to the poor.

933. la quarte ide augusti The month is here given in Latin, as against the French form in l. 746. The date by the modern calendar is August 10.

942. Ou regne The scribe of *A* seems to have understood *Eu regne* or

Eu regné 'in the kingdom'; but the reading of the original is no doubt that preserved by *B*, 'where He reigns' (cf. 74, 949).

    946. tel The correct form is found in *B*; cf. note on l. 314 above.

GLOSSARY

The glossary is selective, omitting words which have the same or similar form and meaning in Modern French, or which are in common use in Old French. An attempt has been made to include all words, forms, or phrases that are peculiar to this text or to Anglo-Norman. Line references are complete unless followed by *etc.* The letter *n* after a line reference indicates that the word is treated in a note. Verbs are normally listed under the infinitive (if no line reference immediately follows the infinitive, this form is not found in the text); isolated verb forms are listed separately. Unless otherwise indicated, nouns are given in the oblique singular form; gender is indicated only if it can be ascertained from the text. Adjectives are given in the masculine oblique singular unless otherwise noted. Orthographical variants are given in round brackets immediately after the headword.

aage, *s.* age 198

aaust, *s.* August 746

afier; *ind. pr. 1* afi 603, 605; *2* afies 600; *v. refl.* trust

aflicïuns, *s. pl.* self-mortification 935

agraventé, *pp.* of **agraventer,** *v.a.* beat to the ground, overwhelm 690

aiglenter, *s.* thorny branches of the wild rose 519, 523

aire, *s.:* **en a.** at once 294

ajoster 530, *v.a.* unite (+ *o* with)

alme (ame), *s.* soul 68, 906

amendez, *imper. 5* of **amender,** *v.a.* correct 16

amenuisera, *fut. 3* of **amenuisier,** *v.n.* diminish 420

ancele, *sf.* handmaiden 76*n*

angoissous, *adj. nom.* anguished 674

angre, *sm.* angel 717

apareiller 361; *pp.* **apareillee** 392; *v.a.* prepare

aperceif, *ind. pr. 1* of **aperceivre,** *v. refl.* perceive, understand 19

apostoile, *s.* pope 86, 243

apostre, *s.* apostle 348

aprestee, *pp.* of **aprester,** *v.a.* prepare, make ready 775

apruef, *adv.* afterwards 621

araim, *s.* brass 435

archangre, *sm.* archangel 776

archidiacne, *sm.* archdeacon 128, 246

ardant, *adj.* red-hot 636, 841

ardor, *sf.* burning 883

ardre; *ind. pr. 3* art 637, 638; *cond. 2* ardroies 877; *pp.* ars 867; *v.a.* burn

aromat, *s.* perfume 915

artimage, *s.* magic 798

asis, *pp.* of **asseeir,** *v.a.* place, put 838

asprement, *adv.* severely 670

atriblé, *pp. adj.* broken, afflicted 849, 853

augusti, *Latin gen.* August 933

avenuz, *pp.* of **avenir,** *v.n.* take place, happen 322

aviler 450; *ind. pr. 3* avile 452; *v.a.* dishonour 450; *v. refl.* demean oneself 452

baptiser; *ind. pr. 3* baptise 294, baptize 734; *subj. pr. 3* baptist 730; *imper. 5* baptisez 714; *pp.* baptisee 372; *v.a.* baptize

beal (bel), *adj.* good, kind, comely 123, 221, 385, 891; *adv.* well 356

bealté, *sf.* beauty 36, 42

beneistre 362; *pp.* beneit 733; *v.a.* bless

besoing, *sm.* task, matter 1, 15; **al b., en b.** in time of need 9, 13

bien, *sm.* good, good thing 55, 311, 338, 379, 446, 511; *adv.* well 19, 81, 106, etc.

bonement, *adv.* in friendly fashion 269

bons, *s. pl.* good people, the righteous 509

catasta, *s.* scaffold or platform used in torturing prisoners 691n, 724

celer; *imper.* 2 ceile 783; *pp.* celez 9; *v.a.* hide

celestien, *adj.* celestial 608

chair; *pret.* 3 chai 708; *pp.* chaue 214; *v.n.* fall

char, *sf.* flesh 503, 639, 794, 884

charbun, *sm.* coal, coals 841, 856, 862, 920

chartre, *sf.* jail, prison 323, 384

chief (chef), *sm.* head 101, 207; headquarters, capital 108

ciu, *adj.* blind 289, 301; *s.* blind person 304

clot, *ind. pr.* 3 of clore, *v.a.* close 914

coivre, *ind. pr.* 3 of covrir, *v. refl.* hide 14n

confondue, *pp.* of confondre, *v.a.* overturn, destroy 213

conmander (commander); *ind. pr.* 3 conmande 204, 207, 518; *pret.* 3 conmanda 537, 725; *pp.* commandé 162, cummandé 381, conmandé 387, 723, 768; *v.a.* order, command; entrust 162, 725

conmoveir 264; *pp.* cummeu 217; *v.a.:* c. en ire, c. a ire anger, excite to anger

contrait, *sm.* cripple 304

copable, *adj.* guilty 943

coroies, *sf. pl.* leather thongs of a scourge; **unes coroies** a scourge 668

corone, *sf.* crown 110

Corpus Cristi, *Latin* Holy Communion 939

costé, *sm.* side 636, 638

coveita, *pret.* 3 of coveiter, *v.a.* desire, covet 260

covient, *ind. pr.* 3 of covenir, *v.n.* be necessary 335

covoitise, *sf.* covetousness 89, 180

creance, *sf.* belief, faith 573, 737, 817

creator, *sm. obl.* 450, 515, 715, 850; *nom.* crieres 468, creator 479n; creator

credo, *Latin* I believe 364, 367

creindre; *ind. pr.* 1 criem 552, 816; 2 criens 811; 3 crient 685, 687; *v.a.* fear

creistra, *fut.* 3 of creistre, *v.n.* grow 419

crier; *pret.* 3 cria 462; *pp.* crié 461; *v.a.* create

crieres, *see* creator

crote (croute), *sf.* crypt 754, 926

cruçun, *sm.* small jug 728

cuer (quer), *sm.* heart 49, 783, 853; **de bon c.** wholeheartedly 80

cure, *sf.:* mettre la c. sur give the responsibility to 131

cuvert, *sm.* scoundrel, wretch 846

cuvertise, *sf.* perfidy, infamy 99

damage, *s.* loss, harm 340

dan(z), *s., title-word of respect* lord 40, 155

debatu, *pp.* of debatre, *v.a.* beat severely 666

debonaire, *adj.* of high birth 281

deça, *adv.* on this side 897

deciple, *s.* disciple 2

decoler; *pret.* 6 decolerent 237; *pp.* decolez 750; *v.a.* behead

defors, *prep.* outside 741

deguerpis, *ind. pr.* 2 of deguerpir, *v.a.* abandon 192

deigner; *pret.* 2 deignas 893; 3 deigna 299, 716; *v.n.* (+ inf.) deign to, have the goodness to

dejoste, *prep.* beside, near 765

delaisser 549, *v.n.* abandon

demenez, *pp.* of demener, *v.a.* lead by force 64

demostrer 790, *imper.* 2 demostre 705; 5 demostrez 15; *v.a. and refl.* show, show oneself

demuert, *subj. pr.* 3 of demorer, *v.n.* delay, be late 52

departira, *fut.* 3 of departir, *v.a.* separate 118

deprier 240, *v.a.* pray to

descreistre 419, *v.n.* decrease, diminish

descrivre; *ind. pr.* 3 descrit 30; *subj. pr.* 3 descrive 795; *v.a.* describe

descuevre, *ind. pr.* 3 of descovrir, *v. refl.* reveal oneself 13

deservir; *pret. 3* deservi 153; *pp.* deservi 902; *v.a.* merit 902; pay back 153*n*

despendu, *pp.* of despendre, *v.a.* distribute 165, 222, 407; pass (time) 821

despoiller 518; *pp.* despoillez 665; *v.a.* undress, disrobe

despit, *ind. pr. 3* of despire, *v.a.* scorn 853

desque, *adv.:* d. a (of time) by 138; (of place) (up) to 390; *conj.* when, as soon as 459

destorber 789, *v.a.* prevent, make difficult

destrait (destreit), *sm.* distress 554, 693

destruire 97, 100, 105; *ind. pr. 3* destruit 103; *imp. 3* destruieit 91; *pp.* destruit 213, 499, 654; *v.a.* destroy

desverie, *s.* folly, madness 881

desvestu, *pp.* of desvestir, *v.a.* undress, disrobe 522

desvez, *pp. adj. nom.* enraged 421, 844

devin, *adj.* divine 810; *s.* theologian 809

diacre (diacne), *sm.* deacon 122, 127, 245

dis, *sm. pl.* days: toz dis always 178

dis, *sm. pl.* words, promises 331

dispersit, *Latin* he distributed 156

doter 340; *ind. pr. 1* dot 607, 660, dout 609; *3* dote 684; *imper. 4* dotun 391; *5* dotez 114; *v.a.* fear, dread

doutrine, *sf.* teaching 375

drap, *sm.* cloak 712; shroud 916

drecier 766; *imper. 5* dreciez 1; *v.a.* build, set up 766; *v. refl.* address oneself 1

dunt (dont), *pron. interr.* with what 21; *rel.* for which 56; of whom 236; of which 943

eé, *sm.* mature years 806

enconbrer, *s.* burden, obstacle 70

encontre, *prep.* against 200, 817

encumbre, *ind. pr. 3* of enconbrer, *v.a.* burden, hinder 21

engin, *sm.* trick, stratagem 71, 798

enluminer 300; *pp.* enluminé 529; *v.a.* restore sight to 300; enlighten 529

enpeint, *ind. pr. 3* of enpeindre, *v.a.* push 12

enquiert, *ind. pr. 3* of enquerre, *v.a.* inquire, ask 261

ens, *adv.:* ens en in (the midst of) 618

ensement, *adv.* in the same way 393

enuint, *ind. pr. 3* of enoindre, *v.a.* anoint

envolepé, *pp.* of envoleper, *v.a.* wrap 916

eschar, *s.* scorn 615

eschever 27; *imper. 2* escheve 588; *v.a.* avoid

escripture, *sf.* scripture, written works 805; sainte e. the Bible, holy scripture 437

escrit 347, 458, escris 568, *pp.* of escrivre, *v.a.* write

escrit, *sm.* observation, statement 3

escumengé, *sm.* excommunicated person 558*n*

eshaucerai, *fut. 1* of eshaucer, *v.a.* raise up, exalt 194

esleeça, *pret. 3* of esleeçer, *v. refl.* rejoice 259

esmaier 102, *v.a.* frighten, dismay

esparpeillent, *ind. pr. 6* of esparpeiller, *v.a.* spread out 842, 857

espirer 336, *v.a.* inspire

espoenter 788, *v.a.* frighten

esprover 8; *pp.* esprové 6; *v.a.* test, prove

esse, *Latin* to be 645

ester 711, *v.n.* stand

estoire, *s.* story, history 77, 84, 377, 805

estreine, *s.* (evil) gift 473

estrif, *sm.* suffering 678

estros, *adv.:* a e. certainly, without question 343

eve, *s.* water 729, 732, 871

evesché, *s.* bishopric 108

fais, *s.pl.* times 368

faisance, *sf.* deeds (collective) 314, 607, 816, 946

faiture, *s.* (man-made) creation 438, 447, 453

feel, *sm.* faithful one 543

felon (felun), *adj.* treacherous, foul 71, 93, 263

fiche, *ind. pr. 3* of ficher, *v.a.* place, put 49

fier, *sm. nom. pl.* proud men 24

figure, *s.:* en f. de as a symbol of, in the name of 369

folor, *s.* folly, madness 81

fors, *prep.* except 55; ne . . . fors only 22

forsené, *pp. adj.* (driven) mad, insane 534, 881

frigerie, *s.* refreshment, comfort 862, 885

funs, *s. pl.* baptismal font 361

fust, *s.* wood 541, (of the tree of knowledge) 496*n*, (of the Cross) 497; **fuz,** *obl. pl.* sticks, cudgels 617

gerdis, *see* **greil**

gieus, *s. pl.* games 763

gloire, *sf.* (heavenly) glory 26, 28, 83, 789, etc.

grace, *sf.* grace 69, 308, 359, etc.; blessing, gift 153; *s. pl.* thanks 302, 310, 619, etc.

greellent, *ind. pr. 6* of **greeller,** *v.a.* grill, roast 843

greil (gredil, gerdis), *sm.* grill 836*n*, 842, 854, 859, 868, 907, 920

gueredon, *s.* reward 747

guerpir; *ind. pr. 1* guerpis 139, 196, 661; *imper. 2* guerpis 424, 594, 798; *v.a.* abandon

hisdor, *s.* horror 887

hisdous, *adj.* hideous 792

ide, *sf.* Ides (of a month) 933*n*

idles, *s. pl.* idols 437

illius, *see* **vidue**

iriez, *pp. adj. nom.* angry 664

jaiole, *sf.* jail, prison 274

jeunesons, *s. pl.:* **faire j.** to fast 934

jovencel, *sm.* youth, young man 712

jovente, *sf.* youth 806

juise, *sm.:* **grant J.** Last Judgement 508

jus, *adv.* down 569

kalende, *sf.* Calends (of a month) 746*n*

laenz, *adv.* within 783

laies, *adj. f. pl.* ugly 673*n*

laminas, *Latin* plates, sheets 631*n*

languissans, *adj.* languishing (on account of illness) 306

las, *s.* wretch 533

lesser 283; *ind. pr. 1* les 202; *pp.* laissé 911, lessé 919; *v.a.* leave, abandon; allow, let

letreure, *s.* writing 804

liement, *adv.* joyfully 394

los, *s.* praise 57

mal, *sm.* misfortune 11; evil 338, 342, 510, etc.; **al m.** in time of misfortune 14; **se prendre mal vers qn.** be angry with someone 168; **maus,** *sm. pl.* unrighteous people 509; sufferings 687

maleuré, *adj.* wretched 880

maltalant, *s.* anger 185, 517

martire, *sm.* martyrdom 18, 64, 218

membre (menbre), *sm.* follower, disciple 91, 158, 165, 430; limb (of the body) 671

memoire, *sf.* memory, commemoration 940; wisdom, good sense 901

mener 570, 727; *ind. pr. 6* mainent 208, 218, 232, 741; *pret. 2* menas 872; *3* mena 275; *6* menerent 257; *v.a.* lead (away), conduct

merci, *s.* pity, mercy 188, 307, 641, 697, 709; **m. Dé** by the grace of God 740; thanks 56, 867

mescreable, *sm.* unbeliever, infidel 429, 683

mescreant, *sm.* unbeliever 250

mescreue, *pp. adj. f.* infidel 826

mesdire 17; *pp.* mesdit 16; *v.n.* make an error, be mistaken

mester, *s.* need 7

morir 143, 657, 780; *ind. pr. 3* muert 51, 517, 615; *6* muerent 24, 50; *fut. 2* morras 176; *subj. pr. 2* muerges 189; *pret. 3* morut 504; *pp.* mors 756; *v.n.* die

moster, *sm.* church 239

mostrer; *fut. 3* mostrera 327; *pp.* mostré 543; *v.a.* show

mu, *adj.* mute 181, 434, 436

muablez, *adj.* changeable, mutable 25

muce, *ind. pr. 3* of **mucer,** *v.a.* hide 409

mué, *pp.* of **muer,** *v.a.* change 338, 357

munt (mund, munde), *sm.* world 25, 45, 87, 465, 468, 647; earthly life 21, 54

neai, *pret. 1* of **neier,** *v.a.* deny 643, 865

nori, *pp.* of **norrir,** *v.a.* educate, bring up 801

nuitantre, *adv.* by night 751*n*

oance, *sf.* hearing: **en comune o.** publicly, in public court 572

obsequie, *s.* funeral rites 755

oes, *s.* use, benefit 164

ohi, *exclamation introducing vocatives* 333, 430, 533, 681, 880

oiant, *gerund:* **o. trestoz, o. toz** in the hearing of all, publicly 417, 423

oils (oilz), *s. pl.* eyes 894, 914

or, *adv. introducing jussive infin.* 782*n*

ordené, *pp.* of **ordener,** *v.a.* consecrate 753

otrage, *sm.* excessive act, offence 278

otrié, *pp.* of **otreier,** *v.a.* grant 401

ovraigne, *sf.* deed, work 57, 67; **tote o.** all (God's) work, i.e. creation 456

paeles, *s. pl.* pans 841

parage, *sm.* lineage, family 277, 799

paralitici, *Latin* paralyzed people 306

parmaigne, *subj. pr. 3* of **parmaneir,** *v.n.* remain 58

pener 592; *pp.* **penez** 63; *v.a.* cause to suffer

peour (poor), *sf.* fear 180, 566, 604

plait, *s.:* **tenir p.** hold court 414

plateines (platines), *s. pl.* sheets (of metal) 634, 650

plumgé, *pp.* of **plunger,** *v.a.* immerse 368

plummees, *pp. f. pl.* leaded, weighted (with lead) 669

plun, *s.* lead 541, 669

plunbatis, *Latin* lead-weighted clubs 666*n*

poi, *sm.* little 20; **a poi ne, por poi ne** almost 517, 615

porpens, *ind. pr. 1* of **porpenser,** *v. refl.* reflect, think 19

preier; *ind. pr. 1* **pri** 60; *3* **prie** 730; *6* **prient** 307; *imper. 4* **prium** 65, 941; *pp.* **prié** 402; ask, request 60, 307, 402, 730, 941; *v.a.* pray to 65

prendre 101; *fut. 6* **prendrunt** 168; *v. refl.* **se p. a** attack

prinseigné, *pp.* of **prinseignier,** *v.a.* make the sign of the Cross over, bless 733

quanque, *pron.* whatever, all that 149, 182, 461, 613, 626, 637, 662

quarees, *adj. f. pl.* cut square 668

quer, *see* **cuer**

quider 596; *ind. pr. 3* **quide** 100; *v.a.* think, presume (wrongly)

quit, *pp.* of **cuire,** *v.a.* cook 897

raimne, *sf.* branch 104

ravun, *ind. pr. 4* of **raveir,** *v.a.* have again, recover 497

refrigerie, *s.* refreshment, comfort 872

rege(h)i, *pret. 1* of **regehir,** *v.a.* confess, proclaim 644, 866

regeneré, *pp.* of **regenerer,** *v.a.* regenerate, cause to be born again 370

regné, *sm.* kingdom 73, 112, 512

renoié, *sm.* traitor, renegade 559

renueve, *ind. pr. 3* of **renover,** *v.n.* be renewed 31*n*

repleni, *pp.* of **replenir,** *v.a.* fill 359

requis, *pp.* of **requerre,** *v.a.* request 332

rest, *ind. pr. 3* of **restre,** *v.n.* be for one's part 828

retraire 81, *v. refl.* extricate oneself

revert, *ind. pr. 3* of **revertir,** *v.n.* go back, revert 47

revunt, *ind. pr. 6* of **raler,** *v.n.* go back, return 46

rostir 889; *ind. pr. 6* **rostent** 843; *v.a.* roast

sacrifier; *ind. pr. 2* **sacrefies** 601; *subj. pr. 1* **sacrefis** 177; *3* **sacrefit** 845; *fut. 1* **sacrefierai** 178; *2* **sacrefieras** 427; *v.n.* make a sacrifice

salter, *sm.* psalter 154, 458

salvere 467, **salveres** 647, *s. nom. sg.* saviour

sarmoner 335; *ind. pr. 3* **sarmone** 109; *v.n.* preach

saut, *ind. pr. 3* of **salir,** *v.n.:* **s. avant** leap forward 708

seeir; *ind. pr. 3* **siet** 767, 787; *pret. 3* **sist** 412; *v. refl. and n.* sit

seigner 362, *v.a.* make the sign of the Cross over, bless

semblant, *sm.* mien, bearing 891

sené, *sm.* senate 170, 413

serjant, *sm.* man at arms 227, 231, 249, 272, 520, 840, 856

seut, *ind. pr. 3* of **soleir,** *v.n.* be accustomed 292

sevras, *fut. 2* of **sivre,** *v.a.* follow 139

sié, *sm.* throne, seat 412, 787; **faire son s.** take one's seat 576

sofrir 782, *v.n.* be patient, wait

sormontes, *ind. pr. 2* of **sormonter,** *v.a.* conquer, surmount 629

soudé, *pp. adj.* melted 669

tant, *adv.* so much 287, 562, 815; so long 286; **t. par** so very (much) 334,

686; *pron.* so much 810; that much 255; **par t.** thereby, as a result 217, 264; **t. cumme . . . , de t.** to the extent that . . . , to that extent, the more . . . the more 198—9

tendror, *s.* tenderness 771

terme, *s.* delay, period of grace 400

termes, *s. pl.* public bath 761*n*, 762

tert, *ind. pr. 3* of **terdre,** *v.a.* wipe away 713

tolir 475, *v.a.* remove, rescue

traire 28; *ind. pr. 3* **trait** 23; *v.a.* draw 23; *v.n.* (+ **a**) seek after, direct oneself toward 28

trametre; *ind. pr. 3* **tramet** 905; *pp.* **tramis** 386; *v.a.* send

tresque, *adv.:* **t. a** (of time) by 140; until 925; (of place) to, as far as 205, 571, 639; *conj.* when, as soon as 460, 706, 784

tressue, *ind. pr. 3* of **tressuer,** *v.n.* perspire 185

tristo(u)r, *s.* sadness 137, 770

umbre, *sm.* shadow 22

unt, *adv.:* **par unt** whereby, by which 499

vaie, *sf.* way, road 53

valeir 597; *ind. pr. 3* **vaut** 43, 44, 45, 104; *6* **valent** 649; *v.a. and v.n.* avail, be of value 43, 44, 45, 597; be worth 104, 649

veer 662, 861; *gerund* **veant** 422; *v.a.* see; **veant Decio** in the presence of Decius 422

vegiles, *s. pl.* vigil 935

ventent, *ind. pr. 6* of **venter,** *v.a.* blow upon 856

verai, *adj.* true 6, 640, 646

vessele, *s.* (collective) plate 148

veue, *sf.* sight, view 295, 791

vicaire, *s.* lieutenant 273*n*

vidue, *Latin:* **illius v.** belonging to that widow 929*n*

vilté, *s.* scorn 591

virge, *sf.* virgin 477, 481, 482, 483

vult, *s.* face 891

ydropici, *Latin* sufferers from dropsy 306

ymage (image), *sf.* idol 209, 211

INDEX OF PROPER NAMES

The names listed include those of persons, places and buildings.[1] The names are listed as written in the text; if Latin inflexions other than the nominative are used, identification of the case is included in parentheses after the entry. Line references are exhaustive except for the most commonly used names, *Decius*, *Deu*, and *Lorenz*; all variations in spelling are included.

[1] The main sources for details on the topography of Rome used in this Index are Samuel B. Platner, *A Topographical Dictionary of Ancient Rome* (completed and rev. by Thomas Ashby, London, 1929), and H. Jordan, *Topographie der Stadt Rom im Alterthum* (Berlin, 1871, vol. 2). This latter work publishes the oldest written topographical sources, viz. the two fourth-century regionary catalogues, the *Notitia Regionum Urbis XIV* and the *Curiosum Urbis Romae Regionum XIV Cum Breviariis Suis*, and two medieval sources, the eighth-century *Einsiedeln Itinerary* and the twelfth-century *Mirabilia Urbis Romae*.

734, (nom.) 531, 949; **Jesu Crist** (acc. and gen.) 326, 363, 710, 731, (nom.) 298, 302, 308, 467; **Jesum Filium Dei** (acc.) 645

Jovis (gen.) 760 Jove, Jupiter; **temple J.** 760 the temple of Jupiter, situated on the Capitol, a short distance from the imperial palaces on the Palatine and from the forums situated at the foot of these two hills. It was the centre of religious and political activity during the republic and the empire. 'To the Romans it was the symbol of the sovereignty and power of Rome, and of her immortality' (S. B. Platner, *A Topographical Dictionary of Ancient Rome*, rev. T. Ashby, Oxford, 1929, p. 302)

Justinus 752, 921, 938; **Justin** 917: a priest

Lorenz 62, 76, 125, 132, 144 etc. Lawrence

Lucillus 288, 293, 297 a convert

Martis (gen.) 205, 209, 215 Mars, the Roman god of war; **temple M.** 205, 209, 215 the temple of Mars. The dedication on Aug. 1, 2 B.C. of the temple of Mars in the Augustan forum was celebrated annually. It was one of the most magnificent temples in Rome. The forum surrounding the temple was used for Roman courts, and for ceremonies granting official honours by the senate. The medieval *Mirabilia Urbis Romae*, however, locates the site of the martyrdom of Sixtus outside the Appian gate by a different temple of Mars: 'Haec sunt loca quae inveniuntur in passionibus sanctorum. 1. Foris portam Appiam ad templum Martis ubi beatus Xystus decollatus fuit . . .' (Jordan, op. cit., p. 615)

Olimpiadis, termes 761 a Roman bath. The existence of *thermae Olimpiadis* remains in doubt, however. Jordan states that the mention of these particular baths is interpolated in the *Mirabilia Urbis Romae* (op. cit., p.

382) since it is not found in the earlier written sources. The name of these baths is found in some of the Latin versions of the legend (for example, in the *P.P.* version — discussed above in Sources — and in the version printed by Söderhjelm, *De saint Laurent*, Appendix I, p. 4, and in that published by Mombritius, *Sanctuarium seu Vitae Sanctorum*, Paris, 1910, p. 94, but not in the version found in Ado's martyrology, published in the Bollandists' *Acta Sanctorum*, Aug. II, 518–19). Nineteenth-century sources place the baths at the site of the present church of San Lorenzo in Panisperna (see Amato P. Frutaz, *Le Piante di Roma*, Rome, 1962, pianta 66). The *Dictionnaire d'archéologie chrétienne et de liturgie* (ed. F. Cabrol, H. Leclercq, Paris, 1925, VIII, 2, col. 1934) states that archaeological investigations at this site suggest there may have been Roman baths there at one time

Romain 690 Romans
Romanus 707, 728 a convert
Rumme 86, 94, 108, 128, **Rome** 762 Rome

Salaria, (porte) 743 the Porta Salaria, where Romanus was executed, still in existence in Rome

Saluste 765 Sallust, Roman historian; **paleis S.** 765 the palace located in the Horti Sallustiani, built by the historian near the Porta Salaria; the estate became imperial property at the time of Tiberius. The Horti Sallustiani were still a favourite imperial resort in the fourth century A.D. (Platner, op. cit., p. 271)

Sanson 41 Samson
Sixte 210, 218, 232, 243; **Syxte** 85, 106, 136, 171, 173; **Syxtus** 93, 125, 177, 195: Pope Sixtus II, A.D. 257–58

Tiberii (gen.) 910, **Tyberii** (gen.) 571: Tiberius, Roman emperor A.D. 14–37; **paleis T.** 571, 909 no doubt

the Domus Tiberiana, the imperial residence built on the Palatine

Tiburtina, in 924, 927 the Tiburtine Gate; it is still in use today, and the Via Tiburtina easily identified. The burial site is beside the Via Tiburtina, outside the gate

Valerien 266, 271, 383, 386, 396, 397, 401, 421, 720, 874; **Valeriens** 757: Valerian, the provost of Decius; historically it was Valerian who was the Roman emperor during the period A.D. 253–259/60, and it was he, rather than Decius of the legend, who was responsible for the martyrdom of Sixtus and Lawrence

Verano, in agro 928 the field beside the Via Tiburtina in which was located the crypt of the widow Cyriaca. The present basilica of San Lorenzo was built on the supposed spot of burial

Ypolite 272, 329, 354, 384, 410, 726, 912; **Ypolitus** 319, 364, 367, 770, 777: Hippolytus, the lieutenant of Valerian

LA VIE DE SAINT LAURENT

Anglo-Norman Text Society
No. XXXIV
(for 1976)